How to Do
Everything™

Microsoft®
Office Online

About the Authors

Marty Matthews "played" with some of the first mainframe computers, and from those to the latest tablets and smart phones, he has never lost his fascination with computers. He has been everything from a programmer to a software company president. Throughout, he has worked to bring others along with him and help them make the best use of all that computers can do. Toward that end, Marty has written more than 80 books on programming and computing subjects, with many becoming bestsellers and receiving many accolades.

His recent books include *iPhone for Seniors QuickSteps*®, *Windows 8.1 for Seniors QuickSteps*®, *Microsoft Office 2013 QuickSteps*®, and *PHP & MySQL Web Development: A Beginner's Guide*.

Carole Matthews has been in the computer industry for her whole career, from programmer to vice president of her family-owned company. For the past 30 years she has authored, co-authored, or managed the writing and production of more than 50 books, including *Facebook for Seniors QuickSteps*®, *Microsoft Office 2013 QuickSteps*®, and *Microsoft Word 2013 QuickSteps*®.

Marty and Carole are the co-creators of QuickSteps® books and live on an island in beautiful Puget Sound, near Seattle, Washington.

How to Do
Everything™

Microsoft®
Office Online

Marty Matthews
Carole Matthews

New York Chicago San Francisco
Athens London Madrid Mexico City
Milan New Delhi Singapore Sydney Toronto

Cataloging-in-Publication Data is on file with the Library of Congress

McGraw-Hill Education books are available at special quantity discounts to use as premiums and sales promotions, or for use in corporate training programs. To contact a representative, please visit the Contact Us pages at www.mhprofessional.com.

How to Do Everything™: Microsoft® Office Online

234567890 DOC DOC 1098765

ISBN   978-0-07-185007-0
MHID   0-07-185007-4

Sponsoring Editor Roger Stewart	**Copy Editor** Lisa Theobald	**Composition** Cenveo Publisher Services
Editorial Supervisor Janet Walden	**Proofreader** Claire Splan	**Illustration** Cenveo Publisher Services
Project Manager Tanya Punj, Cenveo® Publisher Services	**Indexer** Claire Splan	**Art Director, Cover** Jeff Weeks
Acquisitions Coordinator Amanda Russell	**Production Supervisor** George Anderson	**Cover Designer** Jeff Weeks

To Roger Stewart, our editor and friend for more than 25 years

Contents at a Glance

Contents

x Contents

Acknowledgments

Authors are just the beginning of a book, and McGraw-Hill Education adds a number of people to the project, many of whom we do not know, except that they are under the expert direction of Editorial Director Roger Stewart and Editorial Supervisor Janet Walden. We thank them all for their dedication to this book and for the understanding and support given us.

We would also like to thank John Cronan for his many years of working with us and for his help with Chapters 6 and 7 of this book. He has always been willing to step up to any task that needed to be done and has been a good friend for a very long time.

Introduction

Microsoft Office is the most widely and heavily used of all office productivity packages. With the advent of the free Office Online version, this product is available on any device with a browser, including PCs, Macs, tablets, and smart phones. Simply direct your browser to Office.com and open this book.

    How to Do Everything: Microsoft Office Online provides both the novice and journeyman Office user with the tools they need to become quickly productive with the Office Online set of apps. From opening an Office Online app and starting to use it, to creating and formatting tables in Word, building and copying formulas across sheets in Excel, adding animation in PowerPoint, or organizing notes in OneNote, this book provides all of the steps with many illustrations showing how to do it.

How Should Readers Use This Book?

This book is intended to be a reference rather than a step-by-step guide; use it to get information quickly and completely. When you have a question, want to get a deeper understanding of an app, or just want an overview of an online app, use this book to gain the knowledge you need quickly. This book is for both novices in using Microsoft Office and persons experienced with the desktop version of Microsoft Office but unfamiliar with the online version.

How Is This Book Organized?

Each chapter is organized to give you the essential information on how to use each online app. Here is a brief outline of each chapter in the book:

Chapter 1: Getting and Exploring OneDrive

You'll see how to connect to, sign up for, and set up OneDrive so it will support your needs for online (on the Cloud) storage of files. You'll explore how to use the OneDrive controls, menus, and options effectively, as well as how to set up OneDrive on tablets and smart phones.

Chapter 2: Handling Files in OneDrive

Here you'll learn how to add files and folders, retrieve files, and work with files on OneDrive. You'll see how to open OneDrive files from apps, how to open apps from OneDrive files, and how to share both files and folders.

Chapter 3: Introducing Office Online

You'll discover how to start an Office Online app, both directly and from OneDrive, and then how to locate, open, use, and save an Office Online document. You'll learn how to use an Office Online app's window, ribbon, toolbars, menu, and views, as well as Help, spelling checker, basic formatting, and printing.

Chapter 4: Working with Word Online

You'll see how to enter, insert, and type over text, as well as how to select, cut, copy, paste, and delete text. You'll discover how to move around text with the mouse, scroll bars, keyboard, and the Go To command, and how to find and replace text, count words, and use highlighting.

Chapter 5: Formatting a Document

You'll explore the text formatting tools using the ribbon, keyboard shortcuts, and mini toolbar to apply character formatting, such as font, font size, weight, and color, as well as paragraph formatting, such as alignment, indenting, and spacing.

Chapter 6: Entering, Editing, and Formatting Data in Excel Online

You'll review the Excel data types; how to enter, wrap, and constrain text; how to complete an entry and enter numeric data; and how to enter, format, and work with dates and times. You'll see how to select, edit, copy, paste, and delete data, and how to select, size, add, hide, and remove rows and columns.

Chapter 7: Using Formulas, Functions, and Tables and Organizing Data

Here you'll learn how to reference and name cells and ranges; how to build, edit, copy, move, and calculate formulas; and how to use functions and work with tables. You'll also see how to organize data with sorting and filtering, and how to add, hide, move, and delete worksheets.

Chapter 8: Creating a Presentation with PowerPoint Online

In Chapter 8 you'll create a PowerPoint slide show using templates. You'll also learn to work on an existing presentation, or start one from scratch, adding themes and layouts for professionalism. You'll add content, explore views, and navigate between slides. Finally, you'll add animation, transitions, and SmartArt for interest.

Chapter 9: Working with Slide Content

Here you'll learn how to create notes and comments, and work with text and text layouts. You'll use placeholders and objects to enhance your slide show. You'll use headers and footers, insert hyperlinks, and share a presentation with collaborators.

Chapter 10: Using OneNote Notebooks

You'll create a notebook inserting new sections and pages. You'll add content with images, text, tables, web links, and symbols. You'll explore OneNote views, show authors and page versions, share a notebook with others, check and correct spelling, and print pages.

Chapter 11: Using and Managing Outlook, Calendar, and People

You'll create and send e-mail. You'll see how to display e-mail by arranging, sorting, and filtering it. You'll use one or more calendars to create and track appointments, events, and tasks. You'll manage your contacts by importing or adding people. You'll see how to group your contacts for easier communications.

Conventions Used in This Book

How to Do Everything: Microsoft Office Online uses several conventions designed to make the book easier for you to follow:

- **Bold type** is used for user input.
- *Italics type* is used for a word or phrase that is being defined or otherwise deserves special emphasis.
- SMALL CAPITAL LETTERS are used for keys on the keyboard such as ENTER and SHIFT.
- **Notes** and **Tips** add information related to the accompanying text. They amplify the information, adding points that expand the discussion.

1

Getting and Exploring OneDrive

HOW TO...

- Connect to and sign up for OneDrive
- Explore OneDrive
- Set up OneDrive on your computer
- Set up OneDrive on an iPhone
- Set up OneDrive on an iPad
- Set up OneDrive on an Android device
- Set up OneDrive on a Windows phone

In this chapter, we'll introduce Microsoft's personal cloud computing environment, OneDrive (formerly SkyDrive). We'll talk about how to get and use OneDrive, how to sign up for it and set it up, how to use its basic features, and how to set it up from various devices.

But first, we provide a brief introduction to the cloud.

Explore the Cloud

So what is the *cloud*? In its simplest form, the cloud is the Internet. The Internet is a network connecting millions of computers worldwide. When someone says they are "saving a file on (or to) the cloud," they are using the Internet to connect to another computer where the file is being saved. The phrase "cloud computing" means that you use the Internet to connect to another computer on which you run an application, or *app*. Microsoft OneDrive is a cloud computing implementation with cloud storage and access to the Office Online apps. You connect to OneDrive over the Internet and use the Office Online apps (such as Word and Excel) in your Internet browser, where you can save your files either on OneDrive (on the cloud) or on your own computer.

So why should you use the cloud for storing files or using online apps? There are a number of reasons that will have varying degrees of importance to you. These include the following:

- **Safety** If you store files on the cloud and something happens to your computer, you will still have the files on the cloud (although it is possible, but not probable, for the cloud service to be hacked).
- **Portability** You can go to any computer connected to the Internet and access the files you have stored on the cloud and use the same apps that are available there.
- **Sharing** You can share specific files you have stored on the cloud with anyone you choose by giving them permission to access those files only.
- **Collaboration** In the Office Online apps, you can work together with other people on a document and immediately see the changes others have made.
- **Convenience** You easily can create and access your files from a number of devices, including smart phones and tablets, which do not have very large storage capabilities and on which you do not have to install the full program.
- **Space** If you are running low on space to store your files, cloud storage can give you additional space—but after a while at a price.

Cloud computing is the latest "hot thing" in computing, but in actuality it is an old concept dating back to the 1960s. The first mainframe computers of the 1950s could run one program at a time. Soon they could run multiple programs at a time (multitasking), and students and business people could submit their computer jobs remotely (remote job entry, or RJE). Soon terminals were connected to the computers and people could fully operate a share of the computer from their terminal (timesharing). Conceptually, there is little difference between timesharing of 1965 and cloud computing of 2015. Of course, the connection today is via the Internet, with programs and storage available from anywhere in the world, generally at a fast speed, and with many, many times the capability of the computers of 1965.

Get Started with OneDrive

To use OneDrive, you first need to have a connection to the Internet. You probably already have such a connection, but if you don't, you can easily get one from your telephone company, cable TV company, cell phone company, or an independent Internet service provider (ISP). Also, you can often freely use the Internet connections provided via Wi-Fi in libraries, coffee shops, hotels, airports, and many other establishments.

Connect to and Sign Up for OneDrive

Once you have an Internet connection, connecting to OneDrive is easy. Here are the steps:

1. Start your computer, if it isn't already running, and start your Internet browser by clicking or double-clicking it. It can be any browser, including Internet Explorer, Firefox, Chrome, Safari, or Opera.

2. When the browser opens, click in its address bar, type **onedrive.com**, and press ENTER. The OneDrive sign-in screen will be displayed. Figure 1-1 shows one of several possible OneDrive opening screens.

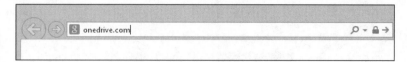

3. If you already have a Microsoft account, click Sign In. If you don't have a Microsoft account, click Sign Up.
4. If you need to sign up, fill in the form and carry out the various verification steps.
5. When you are signed up and/or have a Microsoft account, after you click Sign Up, the Sign In screen is displayed. Enter your ID and password and click Sign In. The main OneDrive screen that is displayed is shown in Figure 1-2.

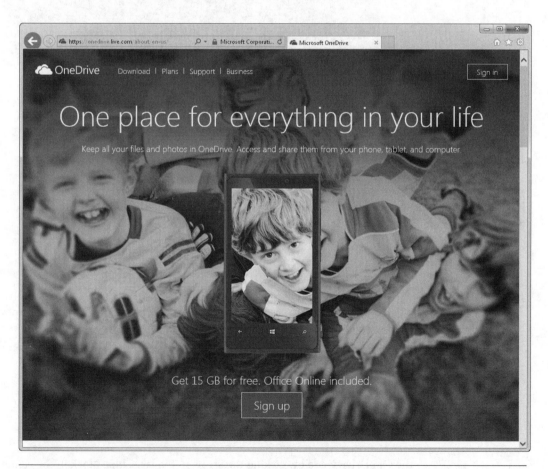

FIGURE 1-1   From the OneDrive opening screen, you can sign in or sign up.

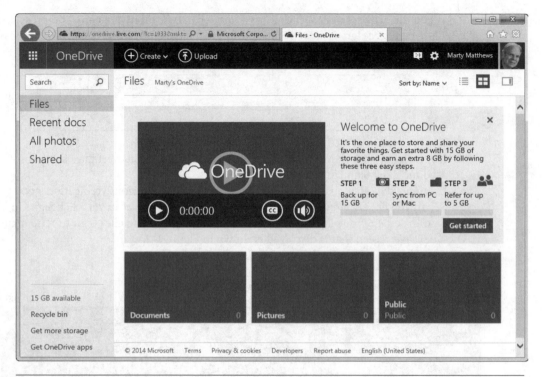

FIGURE 1-2   Your initial view of OneDrive is of file folders for storing documents, pictures, and public items.

 If you have used SkyDrive or OneDrive in the past and/or already have a Microsoft, Hotmail, Live, Xbox, or Outlook.com account, you will have a slightly different screen image and sign-in regimen.

Explore OneDrive

Using OneDrive, you can store up to 15GB for free and access it from any computer or device connected to the Internet. Although OneDrive's basic purpose is to store files and folders on the cloud (actually Microsoft's servers), it does that and much more, and it includes a number of controls and features to facilitate this. Read the next sections to take a tour of OneDrive and explore its controls and features.

Welcome to OneDrive

To get started exploring OneDrive, follow these steps:

1. Watch the OneDrive video by clicking the arrow in the large blue block in the center of the screen.

2. Click Get Started on the right of the Welcome To OneDrive section. From here you can do the following. (If you previously used SkyDrive or OneDrive, the Welcome To OneDrive section may not be available to you.)

   • Sync photos from your smart phone by downloading the OneDrive app for your device from the store. Click Next.

   • Automatically sync files from your computer, tablet, and smart phone by downloading the apps for those devices. Click Next.

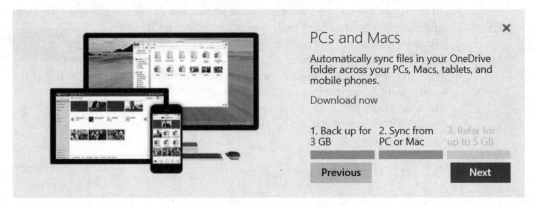

   • Earn more storage space by referring friends to OneDrive. Click Close.

OneDrive enables you to do on the Internet many of the things that you used to do all within your computer. When working with OneDrive, keep in mind that you are in your browser and on the Internet, so operations may take a little longer to complete than they would if you were just using your computer.

Review the OneDrive Controls

Look next at the controls on the OneDrive screen.

1. At the top-left of the screen, click the Office apps icon on the left of the word "OneDrive." This displays the cloud computing apps that are available through OneDrive, as shown next. We'll explore many of these apps throughout this book.

2. Click anywhere in the OneDrive screen outside of the apps display to close that display.
3. At the top of the screen, click the Create plus symbol or down arrow to open a menu of items you can create in OneDrive. In Chapter 2, we'll talk about folders, and in the remaining chapters we'll talk about the other options in the menu.

   Note that if you took time to explore OneDrive before getting to this point, your screen may not look exactly like Figure 1-2 and the Create menu may not be displayed. In this case, click the OneDrive icon at the upper-left corner to return to the correct location.

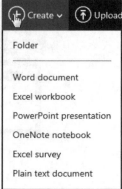

4. Click Upload at the top of the screen to open the File Explorer, where you can choose a file to upload to OneDrive, as shown next. Chapter 2 will tell you about uploading files and other file operations in OneDrive.

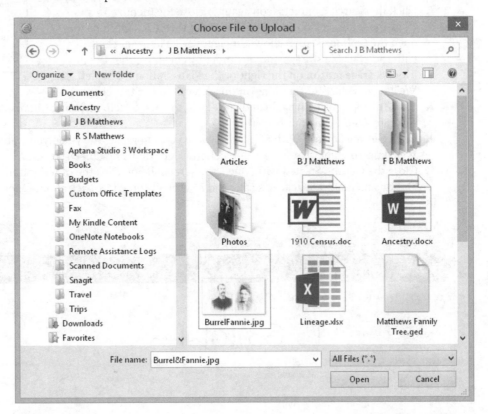

5. Click Cancel to close the File Explorer.
6. Click the Search Contacts icon (the smiley face) in the upper right of the OneDrive screen to open another menu, where you can search your contacts, and search on other networks.

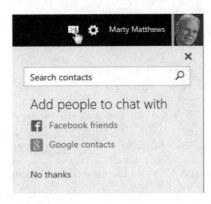

Note that if you have used SkyDrive and/or OneDrive and have used Skype, you may see the names and images of people you have contacted in Skype or other networks.

7. Click the Search Contacts icon again to close the menu.
8. Click the Options icon (the gear icon), and then click Options to open the Options screen shown in Figure 1-3. Here you can work with the available storage and buy more by clicking either the Buy More Storage button on the right or the Plans option on the left. We'll review the other options on this screen later in this chapter.
9. Click the Options icon again and click Help to open a Help screen at Microsoft.com in a separate window in your browser.
10. Click Getting Started With OneDrive. Here you can replay the video you watched in the Welcome To OneDrive section and get other tips on using OneDrive.
11. Close the Getting Started with OneDrive screen. If you click the other option on the Options menu, Feedback, you can send Microsoft some feedback about OneDrive.

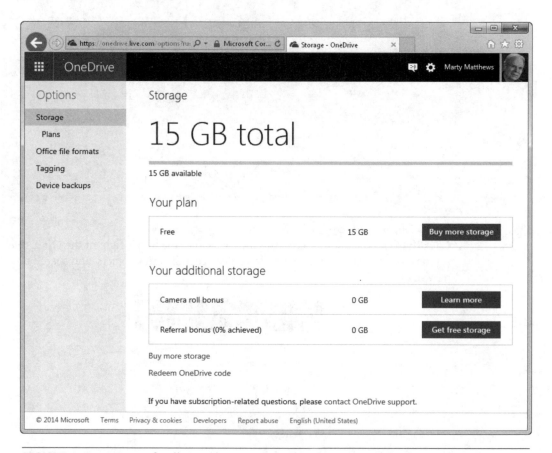

FIGURE 1-3 Microsoft tells you the amount and components of the free storage you are given.

12. Click the OneDrive icon at the upper left to return to the OneDrive screen.
13. At the far right of the second row of options on the screen are several icons that enable you to arrange the folders on the OneDrive screen.

- Clicking the icon in the middle (the default) displays folders as blocks, as shown in Figure 1-2 earlier in this chapter.
- Clicking the icon on the left displays folders in a list, as shown in Figure 1-4.
- Clicking the icon on the right opens a detail pane in which the selected file is displayed along with its sharing status and other information. You'll see examples of this in Chapter 2. Click the icon again to close the pane.

 The best way to get more cloud storage space is to purchase an annual subscription to Office 365, especially if you think you need Office 365 anyway.

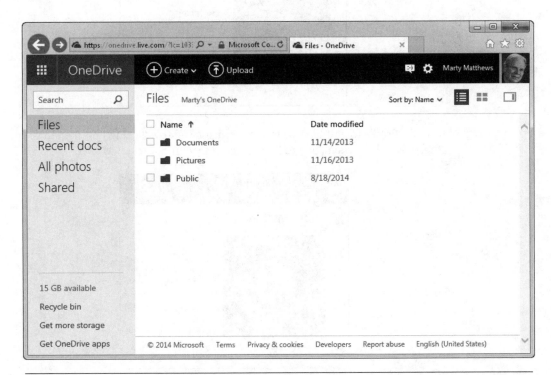

FIGURE 1-4   OneDrive provides folder and file views similar to what you can see in the File Explorer.

Set Up OneDrive on Your Computer

As with any new computer application, you want to review how OneDrive is set up and make changes that reflect your tastes. You can set personal options in three areas in OneDrive: the Personal menu, the Options menu, and the Language menu. We'll look at all three of these next.

Personal Menu

The Personal menu (your name) in the upper-right corner of the OneDrive screen is the starting place for setting up OneDrive.

1. Click the Personal menu to display several options. Your first option is to select whether you are shown as Available or Invisible to others who visit your OneDrive page.

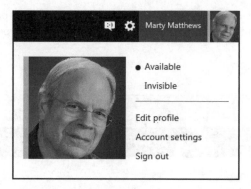

2. Click Edit Profile to edit how your name is displayed (by clicking Edit next to your name). Click Save when you are finished editing your name.

3. Click Change Picture and click Browse to look through your files to locate a picture you want to use. After you have selected a photo, you can drag and/or resize it in the box on the right.

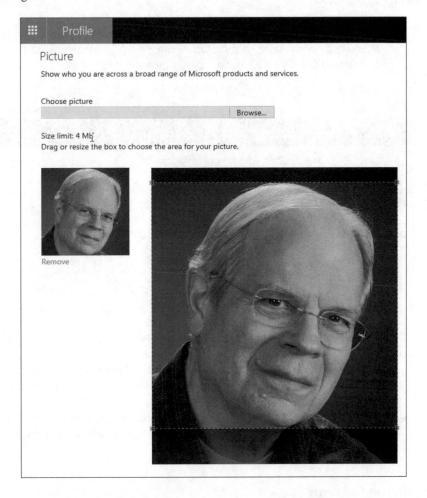

4. When you are happy with the picture, click Save. Then click the down arrow to the right of the word "Profile" and click OneDrive to return to the main OneDrive screen.
5. Click the Personal menu and click Account Settings. Enter your password, and click Sign In. This opens your Microsoft Account detail information. Here you can review and change the personal information that Microsoft has stored about you. Close the Microsoft Account screen when you are finished.

Sign Out of OneDrive   When you are done using OneDrive, it is beneficial to close it for safety reasons and to unclutter your desktop. To do that, click the Personal menu and click Sign Out to sign out (note that this signs out the person who last signed in). At this point, you can either exit OneDrive or sign in again; or, if you are sharing a computer with someone else, the other person can sign in.

Options Menu

The Options menu (the gear icon) towards the right of the screen provides the second area for setting up OneDrive.

1. Click the Options menu and then click Options. On the left, click Office File Formats to choose how you want to store Office documents. The default and normal setting is Microsoft Office Open XML Format, as shown next:

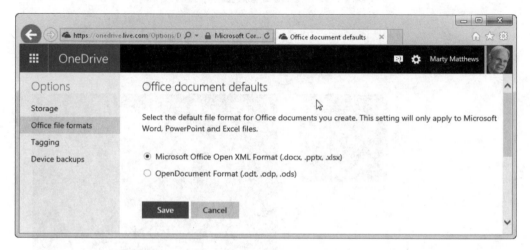

2. Click Tagging on the left to select who is allowed to tag photos of you stored on OneDrive and who can tag others in photos in your photo albums. (Of course, people must first have permission to view any photos on your OneDrive site.) You can allow friends who visit your site to tag photos or set this up so that only you can tag people. Click Save when you have finished with tagging.
3. The final Options menu option is Device Backups. If you use other devices, smart phones, tablets, and other computers, you can control how information on those devices is backed up to OneDrive.

Language Menu

At the bottom center of the OneDrive screen, click the currently selected language to display a list of language options from which you can choose. When you have chosen the language that you want to use, click Save.

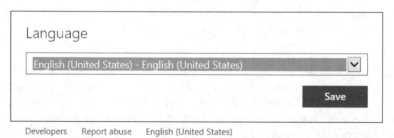

Set Up OneDrive on Multiple Devices

So far in this chapter, the discussion and illustrations have focused on using OneDrive on a Windows computer. One of the major benefits of OneDrive is that you can use it and access your files on a number of other devices. Here we'll briefly look at how to set up OneDrive on an iPhone, an iPad, an Android phone, an Android tablet, and a Windows phone. (Setting up OneDrive on a Windows tablet is basically the same as setting it up on a Windows computer.)

Set Up OneDrive on an iPhone

Before you set up OneDrive on an Apple iPhone, you need to open the App Store and select and install the OneDrive app.

1. From the Home screen, tap App Store, tap Search at the bottom of the screen, tap in the search box, type **Microsoft OneDrive**, and tap Search.
2. When the OneDrive app is displayed, tap Free, enter your Apple iTunes password, and tap Install. When the download has completed, tap Open.

3. Tap Sign In, enter your account user name and password, and again tap Sign In.

4. You are asked if you want to back up your iPhone camera on OneDrive. If you want to do this, tap Turn On; if you don't want to do this, tap Not Now. The OneDrive folders will be displayed.

5. At the bottom of the screen, tap the following:

   - **Backup**   To see the images you have backed up on OneDrive
   - **Recent**   To see the recent files you have sent to OneDrive
   - **Shared**   To see the files or folders you have shared on OneDrive
   - **Settings**   To open the Settings screen and make any needed adjustments

Set Up OneDrive on an iPad

Before you set up OneDrive on an Apple iPad, you need to open the App Store and select and install the OneDrive app.

1. From the Home screen, tap App Store, tap Search at the bottom of the screen, tap in the search box, type **Microsoft OneDrive**, and tap Search.
2. When the OneDrive app is displayed, tap Free. When the download has completed, tap Open.

3. Tap Sign In, enter your account user name and password, and again tap Sign In.

4. You are asked if you want to back up your iPad camera on OneDrive. If you want to do this, tap Turn On. If you don't want to do this, tap Not Now. The familiar OneDrive folders will be displayed.

5. At the bottom of the screen, tap the following:
   - **Backup**   To see the images you have backed up on OneDrive
   - **Recent**   To see the recent files you have sent to OneDrive
   - **Shared**   To see the files or folders you have shared on OneDrive
   - **Settings**   To open the Settings screen and make any needed adjustments

Set Up OneDrive on an Android Phone

Before you set up OneDrive on an Android phone, you need to open the Play Store and select and install the OneDrive app.

1. From the Home screen, tap Play Store, tap Search (the magnifying glass) at the top of the screen, tap in the search box, type **OneDrive**, and tap Search.

2. When the OneDrive app is displayed, tap INSTALL. When the download has completed, tap Open.

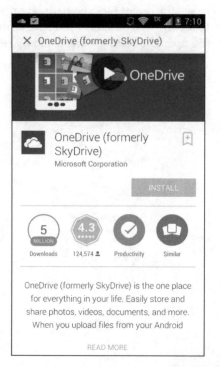

3. Tap Sign In, enter your account user name and password, and again tap Sign In.

4. You are asked if you want to back up your phone's camera on OneDrive. If you want to do this, tap Turn On. If you don't want to do this, tap Not Now. The familiar OneDrive folders will be displayed.

5. Tap the "hamburger" icon (the parallel horizontal bars) in the upper-left corner of the screen:

   - **Camera Backup** Shows the photos you have backed up on OneDrive
   - **Recent Documents** Shows the recent files you have sent to OneDrive
   - **Shared** Shows the files or folders you have shared on OneDrive

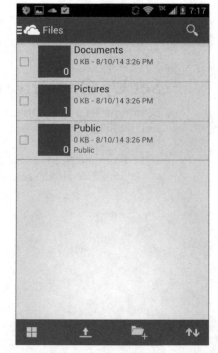

6. Tap the phone's settings icon at the bottom-left, and tap Settings to open the Settings screen and make any needed adjustments.

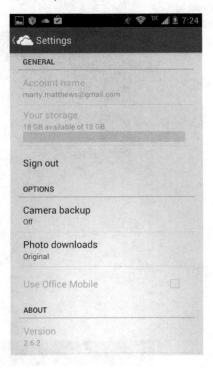

Set Up OneDrive on an Android Tablet

Before you set up OneDrive on an Android tablet, you need to open the Play Store and select and install the OneDrive app.

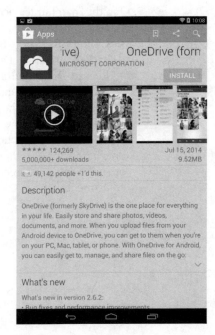

1. From the Home screen, tap Play Store, tap Search (the magnifying glass) at the top of the screen, tap in the search box, type **OneDrive**, and tap Search.
2. When the OneDrive app is displayed, tap INSTALL. When the download has completed, tap Open.
3. Tap Sign In, enter your account user name and password, and again tap Sign In.

4. You are asked if you want to back up your tablet's camera on OneDrive. If you want to do this, tap Turn On. If you don't want to do this, tap Not Now. The familiar OneDrive folders will be displayed.

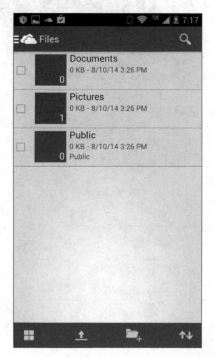

5. Tap the "hamburger" icon (the parallel horizontal bars) in the upper-left corner of the screen:
   - **Camera Backup** Shows the photos you have backed up on OneDrive
   - **Recent Documents** Shows the recent files you have sent to OneDrive
   - **Shared** Shows the files or folders you have shared on OneDrive
6. In the OneDrive app, tap the three connected dots in the upper-right corner and tap Settings to open the Settings screen and make any needed adjustments.

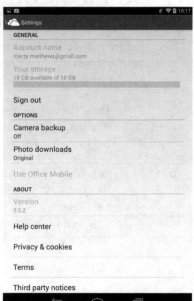

Set Up OneDrive on a Windows Phone

Before you set up OneDrive on a Windows phone, you need to open the Store and select and install the OneDrive app.

1. From the Home screen, locate and tap Store, tap Search at the bottom-center of the screen, type **OneDrive**, tap Search, and tap OneDrive.
2. When the OneDrive app is displayed, tap Install. When the download has completed, tap OneDrive.
3. Tap Sign In, enter your account user name and password, and again tap Sign In. The familiar OneDrive folders will be displayed.

4. At the top of the screen in the title line, tap
   - **Recent**   To see the recent files you have sent to OneDrive
   - **Shared**   To see the files or folders you have shared on OneDrive
5. At the bottom of the screen, tap
   - **Add (plus sign)**   To add files to OneDrive
   - **Thumbnails (little boxes)**   To go to the blocks view
   - **Select (checklist)**   To delete, move, share, and rename the selected files
   - **Search (magnifying glass)**   To search OneDrive for a file

6. Tap the Menu icon (the three dots), and then tap
   - **Create** To create a new folder
   - **Refresh** To refresh the screen
   - **Sort** To sort the files
   - **Settings** To open the Settings screen and make any needed adjustments.

2

Handling Files in OneDrive

HOW TO...

- Add files and folders to OneDrive
- Handle files and folders in OneDrive
- Use OneDrive from apps
- Open apps from OneDrive files
- Share OneDrive files and folders

OneDrive's initial and still major purpose is the storing of files, which can include written documents, such as those produced with Word, Excel, PowerPoint, and OneNote; drawings, such as those produced with Adobe Photoshop, CorelDRAW, and Adobe Illustrator; pictures that you shoot, download, or receive in e-mail; videos from whatever source; audio files; and really any file you can store on your computer. In this chapter we'll look at handling files on OneDrive, including moving files to OneDrive; accessing files that are stored there; copying, moving, and deleting files on OneDrive; accessing OneDrive files from apps; and, finally, sharing OneDrive files.

We'll first look at using OneDrive by itself and then we'll look at using OneDrive with other apps.

 Note When we talk about a "computer," we are referring to any computing device including desktops, laptops, tablets, and smart phones that can run OneDrive, as discussed in Chapter 1.

Work with Files and Folders in OneDrive

If you think of OneDrive as just another disk drive on your computer, you can't go wrong. Microsoft has gone a long way to make that statement true. Pretty much anything you can do on your computer's hard drive, you can do on OneDrive. Whether you use OneDrive alone or with other apps, the process is not much different from using a hard drive.

Add Files and Folders to OneDrive

You can add files to OneDrive by retrieving them using OneDrive or by starting on your computer in the File Explorer and moving files to OneDrive. In either case, you may want to add more folders in which to store and organize your files.

 We use the terms "click" and "choose" throughout to indicate selecting something on the screen, including what you would "tap" with your finger on a touch screen.

Add Folders to OneDrive

You can add folders to segment the file structure and make finding a file easier. It is strongly recommended that you add folders to OneDrive, as you probably have done on the hard drive on your computer. Folders can be added at the top level, as shown in Figure 2-1, and within the three default folders: Documents, Pictures, and Public. You can also add subfolders within the folders you create. The file structure you build is the one that makes sense to you and what you do on the computer. You might add folders at the top level if the current Documents, Pictures, and Public folders ("Public" might be named "Projects" if you have used SkyDrive in the past) are not specific enough for you, if there are particular areas with which you often work, or if you want to store both documents and pictures at a top-level folder.

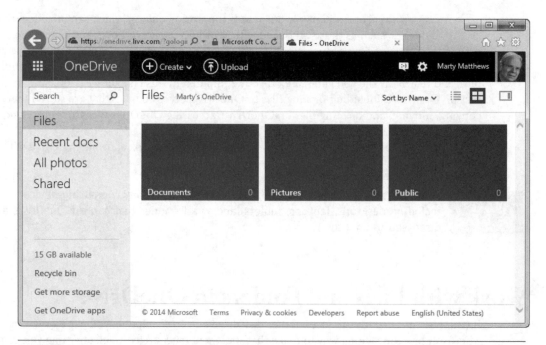

FIGURE 2-1 In terms of file handling, OneDrive operates almost exactly the same as a hard drive on your computer.

Use the Public folder to store files that you want to share with others.

For example, if you work a lot in genealogy you may want to store a number of different files that relate to it, including both documents and pictures, in one folder named "Genealogy," possibly containing subfolders. In this case a Genealogy folder would be at the top level and within that folder there may be subfolders for each of your parents. Also, within Documents, you might have folders for different projects you are working on. Finally, within Pictures, you might have a date segmentation to keep track of images.

The following steps show how you might set up a OneDrive folder structure to accommodate such a folder structure:

1. If OneDrive is not open on your computer, open it now by starting your browser, typing **onedrive.com** in the address bar, and pressing ENTER.
2. If your OneDrive screen does not look like Figure 2-1, click Files in the left column; if your screen is in detail view, click the thumbnail view to reset it.
3. Click Create | Folder, type a name for the folder—in this case, type **Genealogy** for the top-level folder—and then click Create.

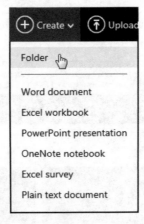

4. To start adding folders within your new folder, click that folder to open it.
5. Click Create | Folder, type a name for the folder, and click Create. Do this as many times as needed to create the subsidiary folders you want—see Figure 2-2. In this case, you would have typed your parents' names, for example, **RS Matthews** for the first subfolder and **JB Matthews** for the second.
6. Click Files in the left column to reset the screen to the top-level files and repeat steps 4 and 5 to open and add subsidiary folders to a folder, as required.

After you have added the folders suggested here, you should see the evidence at the top level, as shown in Figure 2-3. The number of subfolders contained in a folder will increment as you add folders and is displayed on the top-folder's thumbnail icon in the lower-right corner.

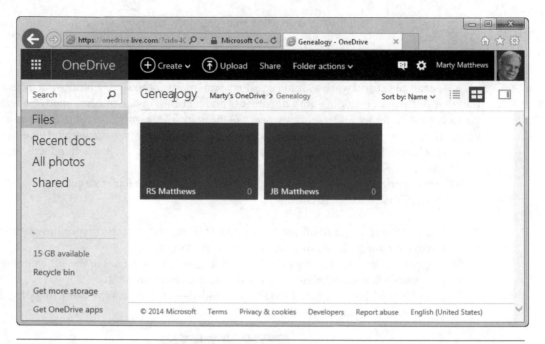

FIGURE 2-2 Creating subfolders for parents within a Genealogy folder

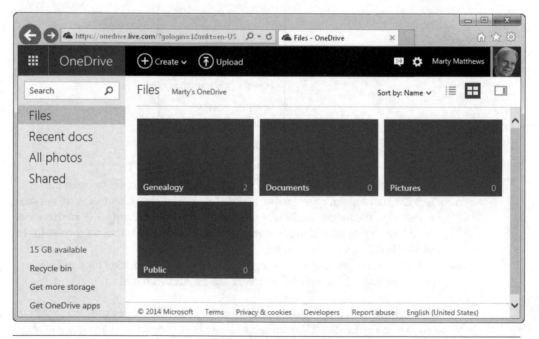

FIGURE 2-3 Your folder structure should reflect how you use OneDrive.

Note You cannot upload or drag a folder to OneDrive. You must create a folder in OneDrive and then upload the contents in the original folder. However, you can upload a zipped folder (with a .zip extension), and you can drag-and-drop files to OneDrive.

Get Files on OneDrive

From within OneDrive, you can upload files from your computer onto OneDrive:

1. Click the folder(s) on OneDrive that you want to receive the files that you upload.
2. Click Upload to open a file or folder selection dialog box, as shown in Figure 2-4.

FIGURE 2-4 Remember that what you upload to OneDrive is a backup copy of what's on your computer.

3. Open the appropriate folders and select the file or files you want to upload (hold down CTRL while clicking to select several files that are not contiguous, or hold down SHIFT while clicking to select the first and last file in a contiguous list). Then click Open.

Note that when you select a folder, a new option— Folder Actions or three dots, if the window is not very big—appears at the top of the OneDrive screen. The three dots are ellipses, which mean that additional options are available.

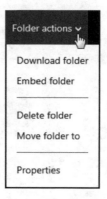

In this case, they are folder actions that you can choose within the current folder, including downloading it to your computer, embedding it in a web page or blog, deleting and moving it, and opening its properties, as shown in Figure 2-5. If the OneDrive screen is fairly large, you will see the actual folder options displayed instead of the three dots or the Folder Actions option.

Place Files on OneDrive

From your computer, you can place files on OneDrive by dragging them and by directly saving them there.

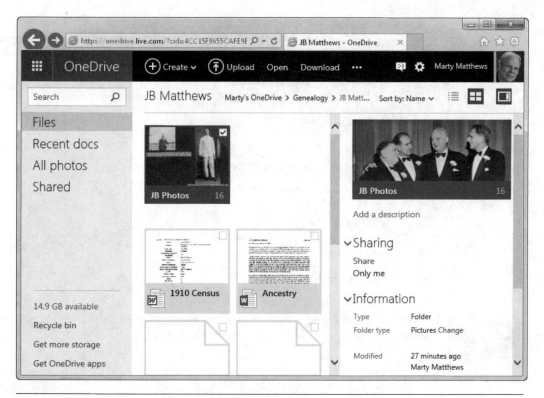

FIGURE 2-5   Folder properties help you keep track of how you are using your folders.

Here's how to drag-and-drop files to OneDrive:

1. Open OneDrive on your desktop. Then, within OneDrive, open the folder into which you want to drag the file(s). Or, if needed, create any new folders.
2. On your computer (this includes tablets and smart phones, where applicable) open the File Explorer and the folder or folders that contain the files you want to move to OneDrive.
3. Select the files (not the folders; remember, you cannot drag-and-drop folders) you want to move and drag them to the open OneDrive window, as shown in Figure 2-6.

Here's how to save files to OneDrive:

1. On your computer, open the app with the file you want to save to OneDrive.
2. Choose File | Save As.
3. In the Save As dialog box, select OneDrive and the necessary subfolders on the left and the final folder on the right in which you want to save the file.
4. Click Open (if needed), and then click Save, as shown in Figure 2-7.

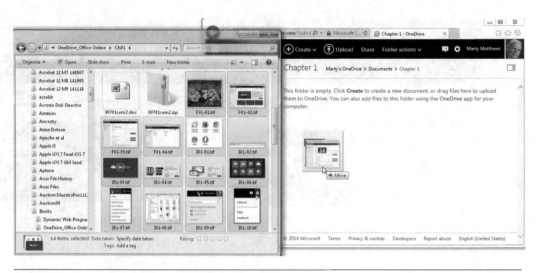

FIGURE 2-6   Dragging files to OneDrive

 Note   In the next chapter, you will learn how you can use Office Online apps as well as regular Office apps to save files directly to OneDrive.

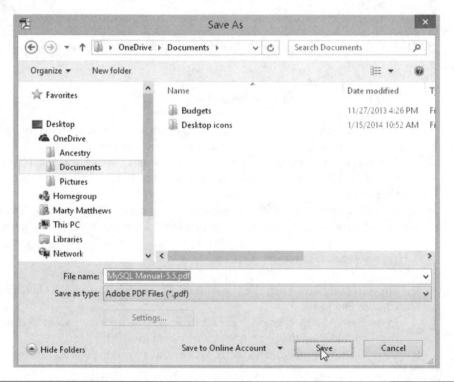

FIGURE 2-7   Saving a file to OneDrive

Handle Files and Folders in OneDrive

Once you get files and folders downloaded on OneDrive, what can you do with them? As with any other disk drive, on OneDrive you can perform a number of tasks to handle files and folders, including rename, copy, move, and delete them. There are some differences between files and folders, and also between document files and picture files, so we'll look at each of these.

Work with Document Files

A document file is any file that is not a picture, a video, or a movie. Document files include Word, Excel, PowerPoint, OneNote, Access, Acrobat, audio, and Zip files, as well as many others. Following are several examples of working with documents files.

1. Open OneDrive in either thumbnail or detail view and open the folder(s) necessary to see the file(s) you want to work with.
2. Right-click that file to open a pop-up menu of tasks you can perform, as shown in Figure 2-8.
3. Click Copy To, to open the list of your OneDrive folders. Click a folder to see the subfolders within that folder.

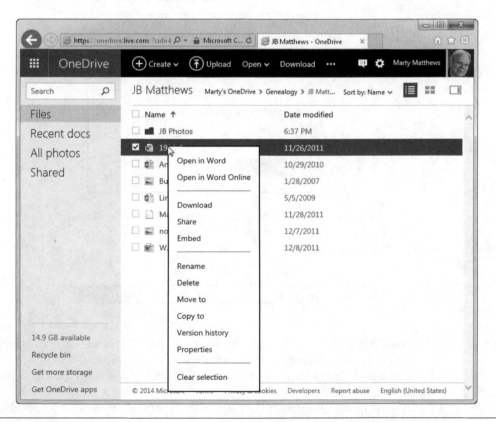

FIGURE 2-8   **You can carry out a wide range of transactions on files in OneDrive.**

4. Click the folder to which you want to copy the file and then click Copy to complete the transaction.

5. Right-click another file to open the pop-up menu and click Move To.
6. Open the folder to receive the file and click Move.
7. Right-click a file you want to delete and click Delete.

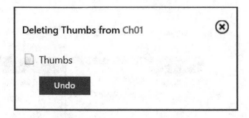

8. If you react quickly, you can click Undo to reverse the deletion.
9. Right-click a file you want to rename and click Rename.
10. Type the new name and press ENTER.

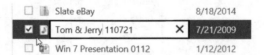

11. Click Open or double-click a file you want to open. The file will open and display in an app. For example, Figure 2-9 shows a file opened in PowerPoint.
12. Right-click a file and click Properties to see the file's properties in the right column, as shown in Figure 2-10.
13. Click the Detail Pane icon in the upper-right corner to close the properties display.

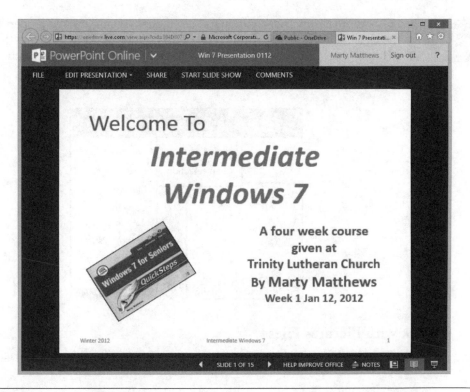

FIGURE 2-9   A number of file types, such as PowerPoint files, can be opened in OneDrive.

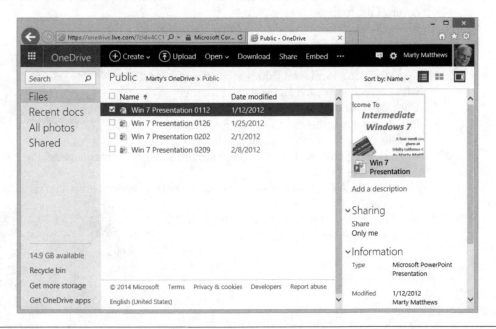

FIGURE 2-10   The display of file properties provides minimal information about the file.

Tip As an alternative to right-clicking a file to open its options and properties, click the check box in the upper-right corner of a file to select it, click the three dots (if the window is small) in the toolbar to open the Other Options menu, and then click Manage to open the familiar set of options to manage the file.

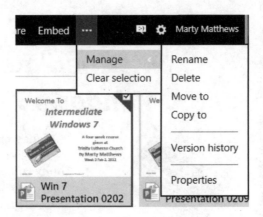

Work with Pictures Files

Managing picture and video files in OneDrive are not much different from managing documents, except that with pictures you cannot create them in OneDrive.

1. In OneDrive, click the folder in which you want to work on a picture file.
2. Right-click the picture file and then click Add As Cover. The picture will appear on the cover of the folder.
3. Right-click a picture file and click Rotate to rotate the picture 90° clockwise or to the right.
4. Right-click a picture file and click Order Prints to send the picture to a local establishment, such as a drug store, where it will be printed and you can pick it up.
5. Click Open or double-click a picture or video file to open it with some options, as shown in Figure 2-11.
   - Click View Folder to return to the folder view.
   - Click Tag Someone to put a square around a face and enter a name. Press ENTER and then Done Tagging.
   - Click Add A Caption below the picture to type a caption. Press ENTER when you are finished.
   - Click the pencil to extract and edit any text that appears on the picture.

FIGURE 2-11   OneDrive allows you to tag people, add a caption, and edit any extracted text.

Work with Folders

Compared to documents and pictures, folders have a reduced set of similar options. You can access the folders either by right-clicking a folder or clicking the check box in the folder's upper-right corner, clicking the three dots in the toolbar (if the window is small) and clicking Manage, or clicking Manage directly in the toolbar. The respective options are shown next, with the right-clicking options on the left, all of which you have seen in previous discussions in this chapter.

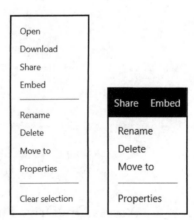

Use OneDrive

OneDrive is an excellent place to store files off your computer, but the purpose of storing the files in the first place is to be able to use them in any way you want. Here we'll look at two important ways to do that—first, from apps that can manipulate the files, and second, to share the files with others.

Use OneDrive from Apps

You have seen how to store files on OneDrive; here we'll look at how to access files on OneDrive from an app to do something with them. Following are two examples of apps opening files on OneDrive. In the remaining chapters of this book, you'll see how Office Online opens OneDrive files.

Access OneDrive Files from QuickTime

Apple QuickTime is a media player used to play music and videos, which you can do with files on OneDrive.

1. Open Apple QuickTime.
2. Click File | Open File.
3. In the Open A File dialog box, from the left side, click Desktop and then OneDrive, and then open the other folders necessary to access the file you want to open.

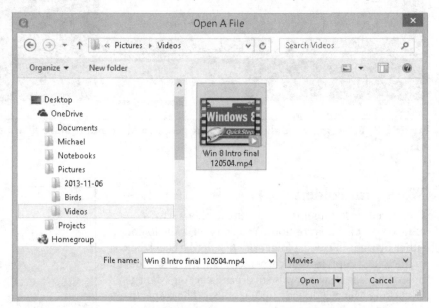

4. Double-click that file. It should open and become available to play in the QuickTime app, as you can see in Figure 2-12.

Access OneDrive Files from Acrobat

Adobe Acrobat and Acrobat Reader are used to display documents in the PDF format, which you can do with files on OneDrive.

1. Open Adobe Acrobat.
2. Choose File | Open.

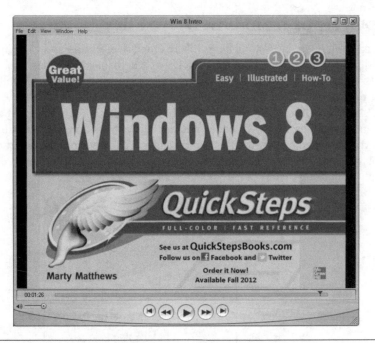

FIGURE 2-12   Most apps can open files in OneDrive.

3. In the Open dialog box, from the left side, click Desktop and then click OneDrive, and then open the folders necessary to access the file you want to open.

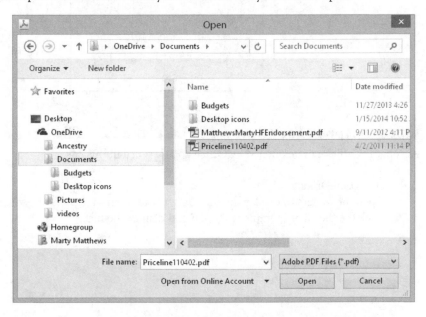

4. Double-click that file. It should open and become available in Acrobat.

Open Apps from OneDrive Files

You can also open apps by clicking a file in OneDrive. Picture and video files are opened and displayed by a player built into OneDrive. Microsoft Office files, such as Word, Excel, PowerPoint, and OneNote files, are opened in their respective Office Online apps running in your browser. You'll see a number of examples of this later in this book. Also, some files not in a Microsoft Office file format can still be opened in Office apps, while other files, such as Zip and audio files, are downloaded and opened by apps on your computer. You can tell which files you can open by viewing them in detail view and determining whether they have an icon displaying their file type. File names with an icon, as shown next, can be opened in OneDrive simply by clicking them.

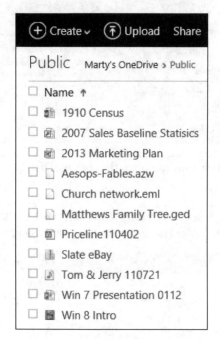

Open an App in Your Browser to Display a PDF File

Acrobat PDF files can be opened by Office apps—Word in this case.

1. Open OneDrive.
2. Open the folders to display the file you want to open—a PDF file in this case.
3. Click the file. Word Online will open and display the file.

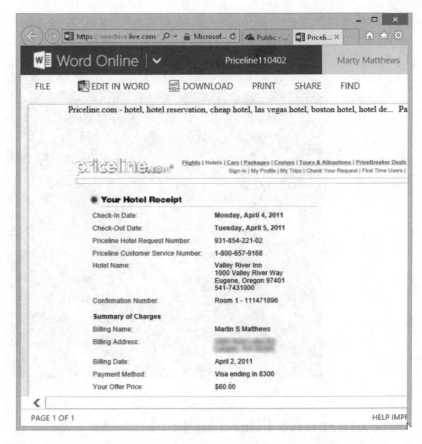

4. Click the Close box (the red x in the upper-right corner) to close the file.

Open an App to Play an Audio File

When you select an Audio file in OneDrive it will be downloaded to your computer and a resident player will load and play the file.

1. Open OneDrive.
2. Open the folders to display the file you want to open—an audio file in this case.
3. Click the file. A message will ask if you want to open or save the file.

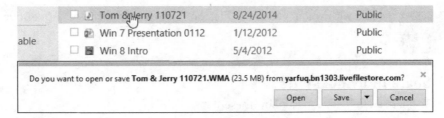

4. Click Open to download the file to your computer, open the necessary app—the Windows Player in this case—and play the audio.
5. Click the Close box to close the app.

Share OneDrive Files and Folders

One of the major benefits of OneDrive is that it enables you to share files with others easily. For example, we work with editors who review what we write and make corrections to our work. We could e-mail chapters back and forth, but if we put the chapters up on OneDrive and share them, the editors can easily work with them there, and we authors can easily go back and review their work, once more on OneDrive. This is especially valuable for this book—with two authors and several editors, all of whom need access to the files. It is also valuable because many of the chapters have many illustrations that are large files, which makes a complete chapter file quite large, sometimes larger than e-mail systems allow. Using OneDrive, we can share a folder, which includes the automatic sharing of all the files in the folder, or we can share individual files, as shown in Figure 2-13.

 People with whom you share files on OneDrive do not need a OneDrive or Microsoft account.

Share Individual Files

To share an individual file, follow these steps:

1. Open OneDrive and the folders needed to see the file you want to share.

FIGURE 2-13   With our book files, we need to share folders that contain all the illustrations as well as the text file.

2. Right-click the file and click Share.

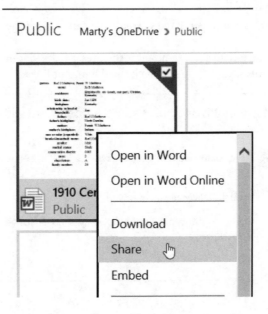

3. Enter the e-mail address for the person with whom you want to share the file, add an optional note if you want, and then click Share.

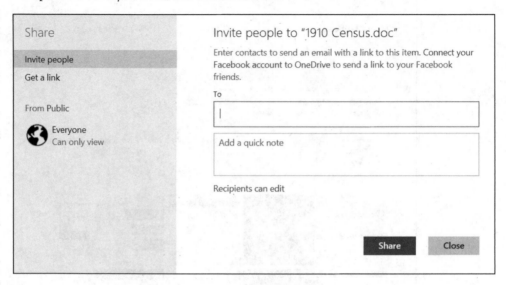

4. You may be asked to complete a security check. If so, click the link, follow the instructions, click Close, and click Share again.
5. You will see a confirmation of the sharing with a note in the right pane that the person you are sharing with can edit the file. If you don't want that, click the down arrow and click Change To View Only.
6. When you are ready, click Close.

Access a Shared File

The person with whom you have shared a file can access it by following these steps:

1. Open the e-mail server and click the message header in the e-mail Inbox.
2. In the message that opens, click the document link.

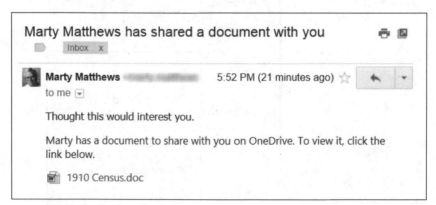

3. If possible—for example, if the document can be opened in one of the Office Online apps—the document will be opened and—if the recipient has the permission—can be edited.

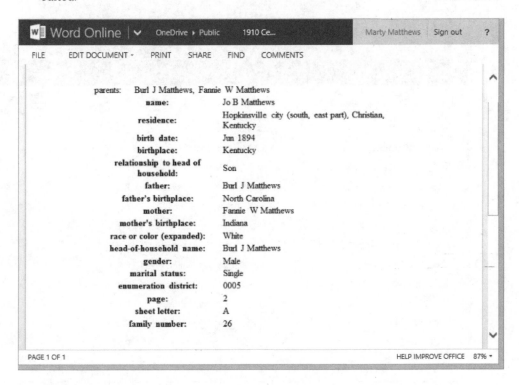

4. When the recipient is done, they can save the document back on one drive for the originator to see and work with.

 When you share a photo or video file, the recipient can view it in a limited version of OneDrive.

Share Folders of Files

Folder sharing is similar to file sharing except that you are sharing a container of files instead of a single file. The recipient can view the files that are included in the folder and open individual files.

1. Open OneDrive and navigate to the folder you want to share.
2. Right-click the folder and click Share.
3. Enter the e-mail address of the person with whom you want to share the folder, add a note if you want, and click Share.
4. If desired, change the permissions by clicking the Recipients Can Only View down arrow and selecting Allow Editing.

The Public folder is automatically shared in its entirety, so if you give someone a link to one file in that folder, they can access all of the files stored there, as shown in Figure 2-14.

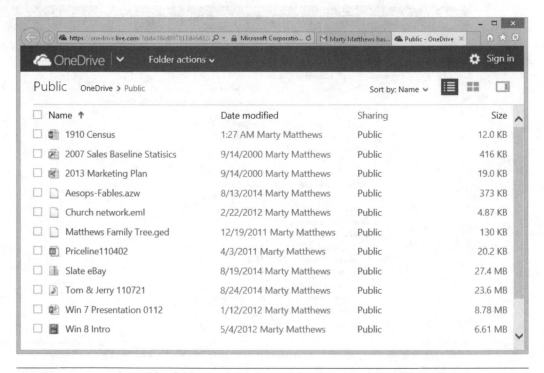

FIGURE 2-14 The Public folder, as the name implies, is open to public viewing.

3

Introducing Office Online

HOW TO...

- Start and close an Office Online app
- Open and save a document in an Office Online app
- Explore an Office Online App Window
- Use the Office Online Clipboard, spelling checker, and Help
- Format, print, and comment Office Online documents

Microsoft Office Online is the online version of the most widely used of all office suite offerings. Most personal computers (PCs) have some version of Office installed, and most people who use a PC probably have Office available to them as well as some experience in its use. Office Online provides the ability to work on Office documents from a browser, on any computer and many smart phones and tablets. If your files are stored on OneDrive, you can use Office Online to work with those files on virtually any computer that is connected to the Internet.

Office Online is both simple to use and sophisticated, offering features that commonly go unused. Office Online delivers a high degree of functionality even when only a small percentage of its capabilities are used. The purpose of this book is to acquaint you with how to use Office Online within four primary Office Online apps: Word, Excel, PowerPoint, and OneNote. You will learn not only how to access the common, everyday features, but also how the many additional features can enhance your experience with Office Online.

In this chapter you will familiarize yourself with Office Online; learn how to start and leave apps; discover how to use the Office Online windows, panes, ribbon, toolbars, and menus; learn how to get help, use the Clipboard, check your spelling, print your document, and customize the Office Online app; and, finally, see how to protect your documents.

In this and the remaining chapters of this book, we talk about using Office Online in a browser on a computer. The type or publisher of the browser really doesn't matter; it can be Microsoft Internet Explorer, Mozilla Firefox, or Google Chrome. In any case, you should be using the latest version, which you can download for free. Also, you can use a variety of computers running a variety of operating systems. We will be using PCs running Windows 8, but this is almost indistinguishable from PCs running Windows 7, Windows Vista, and even

Windows XP. Also, running Office Online in a browser on a PC is not much different from running Office Online in Safari on a Mac. And, finally, using Office Mobile on smart phones and tablets is a similar process as well. The key point is that all forms of the Office apps, be they on a desktop or laptop Windows or Mac computer, a Windows tablet, an iPad, or an Apple, Windows, or Android smart phone, all store their files in a compatible format that can be stored on OneDrive and opened and worked on with any of the devices. This lets you start a document on a desktop Windows computer, work on it with an Apple iPad, and do some last minute tweaks on an iPhone, as you see next, and access and look at it in OneDrive on any device that has an Internet browser.

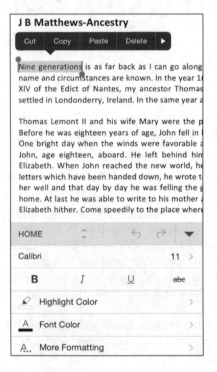

 We use the words "click" or "choose" to indicate selecting something on screen, and we'll tell you to "type" something on a keyboard, assuming you are using a mouse and a keyboard. If you are using a device with a touch screen, you can interpret our instructions for using the keyboard and mouse with the appropriate taps on the screen.

Open and Close an Office Online App

You can open an Office Online app in several ways, from either OneDrive or directly from Office Online. In this section you'll see how to do both, as well as how to exit Office Online.

Start an Office Online App Directly

You can open an Office Online app directly from your browser. Follow these steps:

1. Start your computer, if it is not already running.
2. Open a browser, such as Internet Explorer, Firefox, or Chrome.
3. Click in the address bar, type **office.com**, and press ENTER. Office Online will open, as you see in Figure 3-1.
4. Click the app that you want to use, such as Word Online.
5. Sign in as appropriate for you, and then select the type of and actual document stored on OneDrive or template that you want to use. The app will open, displaying the document or template, as shown in Figure 3-2.

Start an Office Online App in OneDrive

You can open an Office Online app in two ways in OneDrive: by selecting the app you want to use and by selecting the document you want to open.

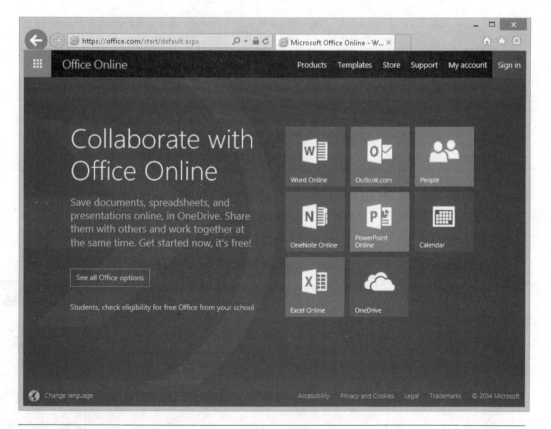

FIGURE 3-1   Office Online provides access to Office apps through a browser on the Internet.

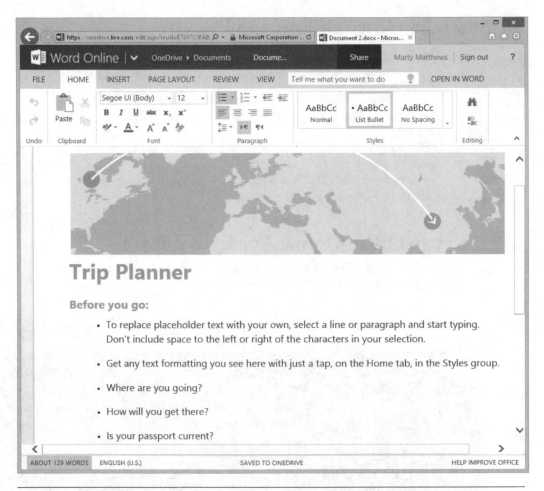

FIGURE 3-2 Office Online provides a number of templates, such as this Trip Planner, that you can use for free to give you a head start on creating a document.

Open an Office Online App by Selecting the App

When you select the app to initially open, you can create a new file to work on in that app. Open a browser, type **onedrive.com**, and press ENTER. OneDrive will open.

1. In Office Online, click Create, and then click the Office Online app you want to use, as shown here. The app will open and display a blank document.

Open an Office Online App by Selecting the Document

When you select a file to work on in OneDrive, it will initially open the Office Online app, but you can choose to edit the file there or in the Office version on your computer if you have that.

1. Open a browser, type **onedrive.com**, and press ENTER. OneDrive will open.
2. Open the folders necessary to display the file that you want to work with, and click that file, as you see in Figure 3-3. The Office Online app will open and display the file you choose.

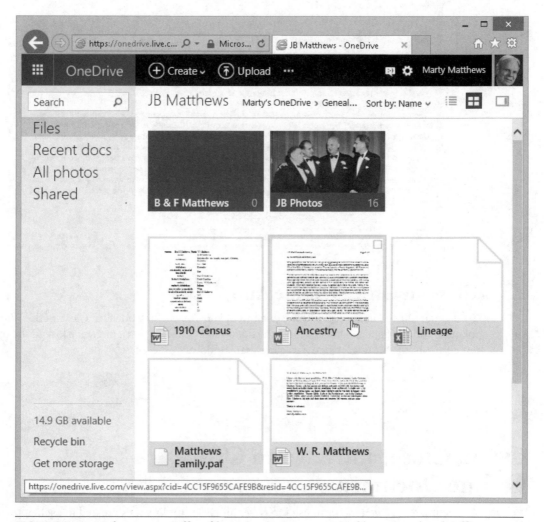

FIGURE 3-3   Selecting an Office file in OneDrive opens the file in the related Office Online app.

3. If you also have the Office app on your computer, click Edit Document to choose whether to work on the document in Office Online or the same app in your computer.

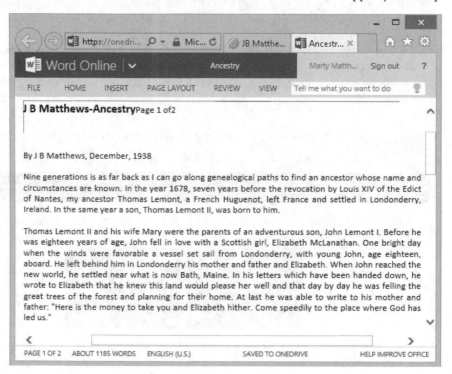

Close an Office Online App

To close an Office Online app and the document you are working on, click Close in the Window's menu bar on the app's tab to close only the document (shown at left), or click Close in the upper-left corner of the browser window to close that window.

Open, Close, and Save an Office Online Document

A "document" is a general term used to cover all Office Online files created in each app—Word documents, Excel workbooks, PowerPoint presentations, and OneNote notebooks. Documents are the medium on which you work and store the results in these apps. They are what the apps produce.

Open a Document in an Office Online App

You may open an existing document or a new one in Word, Excel, PowerPoint, or OneNote in several ways, depending on how you started Office Online.

- If you open Office Online directly and select Word, Excel, or PowerPoint, you are given the choice of opening a new blank document, choosing a template to use to begin a document (see "Use Templates," later in this chapter), or opening a recent document on OneDrive. If you select OneNote, you can open an existing notebook or create a new one.

- If you start one of the Office Online apps by clicking Create in OneDrive without first selecting a document, you'll open the app with a blank document that you can start working on. You may also click File at the top left of the app, which enables you to do the following:
  - **Open a recent document** by clicking a filename under Recent Documents.

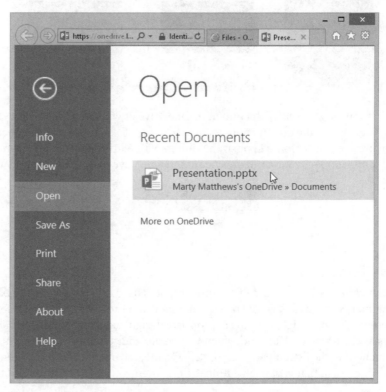

- **Open an existing document, not recent** by clicking More On OneDrive to search for an existing document not recently used on OneDrive.
- **Use a template** to create a new document by clicking New in the left column and clicking one of the templates listed in the right pane.

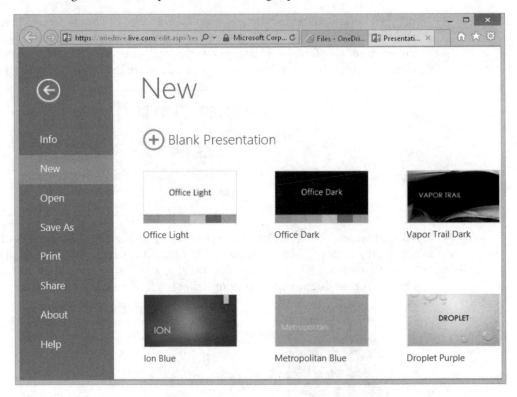

- If you click an Office document in OneDrive, it will open the related Office Online app and display the document in read-only mode. To begin to edit the document in your browser, click Home to open the ribbon with editing commands. If you want to edit in the Office app on your computer (assuming you have one) click Open In Word.

Use Templates

A *template* is a special kind of document that is used as a pattern or the basis for other documents you create. For instance, you might want to create a business letter, marketing presentation, or budget with the appropriate design and format already applied. The template acts as the framework around which you create your document. The template is said to be "attached" to the document. Every Office Online document must have a template attached to it. The document that is opened automatically when you start an Office Online app without selecting an existing document uses a default template that is blank. Other templates can contain boilerplate text, images, design, or formatting options for the types of documents they create; templates can even automate some procedures. Office Online apps offer a number of templates that you can use.

Locate and Open an Existing Document

You may open and work on an Office Online document that has already been created (by you or someone else) in the same Office app whether online or on the desktop. To do this, you must first locate the document and then open it in the appropriate Office Online app. You can either locate the document directly from the Office Online app and search for it there, or upload it from your computer to OneDrive and then open it.

 Not all documents created with a non-Office app can be opened by an Office Online app, although many can.

When you first open an Office Online app, you'll see the Let's Get Started banner. If the file is one you've used recently on OneDrive, it will be listed when you click Recent Documents On OneDrive. If the file has not been opened recently with the app or is not a blank or template-based file, you'll have to go to OneDrive and search for it with these steps:

1. Click Files to display a list of files.
2. Click in the OneDrive Search box (beneath the logo), and type in your search criteria for the file, such as part of its name.
3. Click the search icon (the magnifying glass).

If the file is not available on OneDrive, you will need to upload it from your computer, as described in Chapter 2.

Save a Document in Office Online

As you are working with a document in Office Online, it is automatically saved for you on OneDrive, you don't need to do anything for fear you'll lose your work. You can also download a copy of the document to your computer and save it there if you are working in Word, Excel, or PowerPoint. OneNote Online files are available only in OneDrive.

 As good as Office Online's automatic saving feature is, it is always good to have a backup, so downloading a copy of your file to your computer is wise.

To download a copy of a file you have open in Word, Excel, or PowerPoint Online, follow these steps:

1. Click the File tab in the upper-left corner and click Save As. A list of Save As options will be displayed, as you see for Excel in Figure 3-4. These options will vary depending on the app.

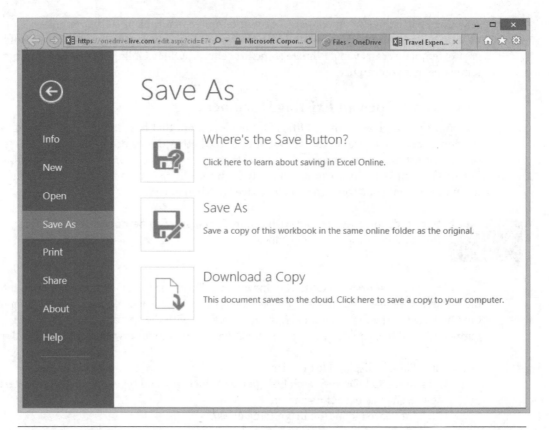

FIGURE 3-4 Office Online documents are automatically saved to OneDrive, but you can also download a copy to your computer.

2. On the Save As screen, click the icon to the left of Download A Copy (or Download depending on the app you are using). You can do the following:
   - Click Open to open the document in the related Office app on your computer (assuming you have the app). From there you can save the document either on your computer or back on OneDrive.
   - Click Save to download the document to the Downloads folder on your computer, from which you can copy or move it to another a disk (including a USB flash drive) or a network location.
   - Click the Save down arrow and click Save, as just explained; click Save As to select a drive and folder in which to download the document, or click Save And Open to download the document to your Downloads folder and open it in the related Office app on your computer.
   - Click Cancel if you do not want to save the document on your computer.

Do you want to open or save **Travel Expense.xlsx** (10.3 KB) from **excel.officeapps.live.com**?

Excel has a unique option not available in the other Office Online apps: it can save a copy of the current document in the current OneDrive folder.

Explore an Office Online App

Office Online provides an assortment of windows, ribbon tabs, toolbars, menus, and special features to help you accomplish your tasks. Much of this book explores how to find and use all of those items. In this section you'll see and learn how to use the most common features of the default window, including the various parts of the window, the tabs on the ribbon, and the task pane. (We are using Word Online for our examples, but most of the Office Online apps are similar. Specific differences in similar apps will be pointed out in the individual app chapters.)

Explore an Office Online App Window

The Office Online window has many features to aid you in creating and editing documents. Figure 3-5 shows an example of what is presented to you by Word (front), Excel (middle), and PowerPoint (back) when you open a new blank document. You can further see the primary parts of the ribbon in Figure 3-6. Although we are using Word as our example, the principal features of the window, including several ribbon tabs, are similar throughout the Office Online apps, so we are describing those common features in this section; specific differences for each app are explained in the corresponding chapters of this book.

 To gain working space in the document pane, you can minimize the size of the ribbon. To do this, click the Collapse The Ribbon icon on the lower-right corner of the ribbon or double-click the active tab name. Click it again to restore the size of the ribbon temporarily, and click the Expand The Ribbon stick-pin icon on the lower-right corner of the ribbon to leave the ribbon expanded permanently.

Understand the Ribbon

The *ribbon*, the container at the top of most Office Online app windows, holds the tools and features you are most likely to use (see Figure 3-6, which shows the Word ribbon). The ribbon collects tools for a given function into *groups*—for example, the Font group provides the tools to work with text. Groups are then organized into tabs for working on likely tasks. For example, the Insert tab contains groups for adding components, such as tables, links, charts, and pictures, to your presentation, spreadsheet, or document. Each Office Online app has a default set of tabs with additional *contextual* tabs that appear as the context of your work changes. For instance, when you select a picture, a Format tab containing styles and tools that you can use with the particular object appears beneath the defining tools tab (such as the Picture Tools tab); when the object is unselected, the Format tab disappears. Depending on the tool, you are then presented with additional options in the form of commands and galleries of choices that reflect what you'll see in your work. Groups that contain more elements than can be displayed in the ribbon include a down arrow that, when clicked, displays these other options.

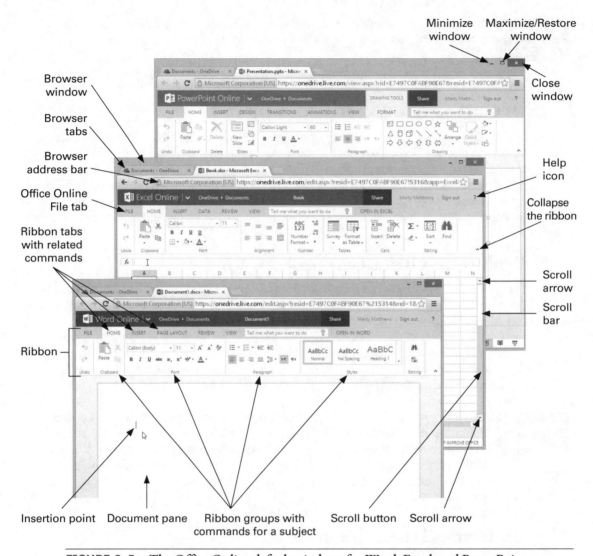

FIGURE 3-5 The Office Online default windows for Word, Excel, and PowerPoint are used for creating and editing documents, spreadsheets, and slide shows, respectively.

Display the Mini Toolbar

When you select text in either Word or PowerPoint Online, a mini text toolbar is displayed that enables you to perform formatting functions directly on the text, such as selecting a font or making the text bold. This toolbar contains a subset of the tools contained in the Font and Paragraph groups of the Home tab. (See "Change Basic Character Formatting" later in this chapter for an explanation of the basic fields and icons in the mini toolbar.)

• Select text by double-clicking it or dragging over the text and the mini toolbar is displayed.

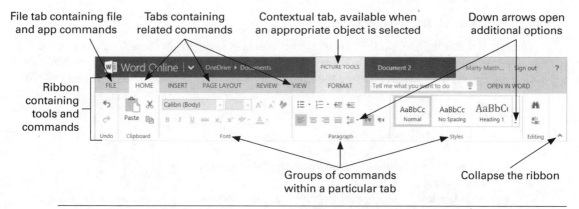

File tab containing file and app commands

Tabs containing related commands

Contextual tab, available when an appropriate object is selected

Down arrows open additional options

Ribbon containing tools and commands

Groups of commands within a particular tab

Collapse the ribbon

FIGURE 3-6   Organized into tabs and then groups, the commands and tools on the ribbon are used to create, edit, and otherwise work with documents.

- Click a button or icon on the mini toolbar that represents the tool to do something. For instance, click B for bold to make the selected text boldface.

The mini toolbars for Word (on the left), PowerPoint (center), and OneNote (right) are shown next. Excel does not have a text mini toolbar.

Use Tabs and Menus

Tabs are displayed at the top of the ribbon or a dialog box. Menus or additional options are displayed when you click a down arrow on a ribbon button or on a toolbar. Here are some of the ways to use tabs and menus:

- To open a tab or menu, click the tab or menu.
- To select a tab or menu command, click the tab or menu to open it, and then click the option.

To help clarify what is said later in this book, some options have dual functionality—that is, you can click the option label to perform the stated action, such as "Click *Labelname*." Or you can click its down arrow to have other choices, such as "Click the *Labelname* down arrow." An example is to "Click Bullets" to assign the standard type of bullet to a selected phrase, versus "Click the Bullets down arrow" to choose the type of bullet.

Use Various Views

Each of the Office Online apps presents documents in several views, enabling you to choose which view facilitates the task you are doing. To access a view, click the View tab and then click the view you want to use. Here are the various views for Word, Excel, PowerPoint, and OneNote.

Word Online

Word provides three possible views:

- **Editing View** Displays the text with the full ribbon and other controls.
- **Reading View** Displays the text without the ribbon or other controls, giving you a larger reading space. Click Edit Document at the top of the window to change back to Editing View.
- **Header & Footer** Displays text boxes for you to enter a page header and a page footer.

Excel Online

Excel displays two possible views:

- **Editing View** Displays the text with the full ribbon and other controls.
- **Reading View** Displays the text without the ribbon or other controls, giving you a larger reading space. Click Edit Workbook at the top of the window to change back to Editing View.

PowerPoint Online

PowerPoint contains five possible views:

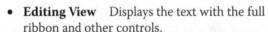

- **Editing View** Displays the text with the full ribbon and other controls.
- **Reading View** Displays the text without the ribbon or other controls, giving you a larger reading space. Click Edit Presentation at the top of the window to change back to Editing View.
- **Slide Show** Displays the slides in a full screen view. Click the screen to go to the next slide or move the mouse to the lower-left corner to display previous, next, and exit controls. You can also exit the slide show by pressing ESC.
- **Notes** Displays a "split" page showing the slide on top and any notes that have been entered for that slide on the bottom. Select another view to leave Notes.
- **Show Comments** Displays real-time collaborative comments on the right of the screen.

OneNote Online

OneNote provides four possible views:

- **Editing View** Displays the text with the full ribbon and other controls.
- **Reading View** Displays the text without the ribbon or other controls, giving you a larger reading space. Click Edit Notebook at the top of the window to change back to Editing View.

- **Show Authors**   Displays the author's name next to the text he or she added.
- **Page Versions**   Displays the versions of the current page.

Use Common Office Online Tools

Office Online offers several common tools and commands among its apps. This section presents the following five tools that you will likely use:

- Help
- Clipboard
- Text formatting
- Printing
- Spell checker

Open Help

The Office Online Help system is maintained by Microsoft. It can be accessed by clicking the Help icon in the upper-right corner of the ribbon or by choosing File | Help | Help to open the app's Online Help window, shown in Figure 3-7 for Word.

FIGURE 3-7   When you click the Help icon, you will see the app's Online Help window, where you can click the topic for which you want help or search for more specific topics.

In the Online Help window, do one of the following:

- Find the topic for which you want help, and click it.
- Type words in the Search Help text box, and click the Search icon (the magnifying glass).

On the toolbar at the top of the Online Help window are several options for navigating and printing the topics, as shown next.

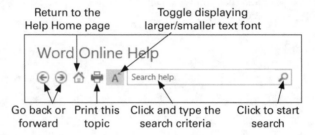

Use the Office Online Clipboard

The Office Online Clipboard is the same in all Office Online products and is located on the left on the Home tab ribbon. You can copy and cut objects and text from any Office Online app and paste them into the same or another Office Online app. The Clipboard can contain only one item at a time.

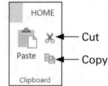

To use the Clipboard, begin by selecting the text you want to work with in your document by double-clicking or dragging over it. You then can use the first two options in the Office Online Clipboard:

- **Cut**   Removes the selected text from its current location and places it on the Clipboard (but you can't see it there).
- **Copy**   Leaves the selected text in its current location and places a copy of it on the Clipboard.

You can then click in the current or another Office Online document where you want to place the text from the Clipboard.

Then click the third option in the Clipboard:

- **Paste**   Copies the Clipboard contents to the selected location, leaving it also on the Clipboard to paste to another selected location.

Check Spelling

The spelling checker automatically runs in the background and flags (with a wavy red underline) as potential misspellings any words that it can't find in its dictionary. A word isn't necessarily spelled incorrectly if it is not found, but it is a possibility that you can check if desired.

the saason

To check an individual word that has been flagged as misspelled, right-click the word. A context menu will display one or more options for correct spellings, as shown here. Click the correct word if it is on the list. If the spelling checker has incorrectly flagged a word as being misspelled, you can click Ignore Spelling Error.

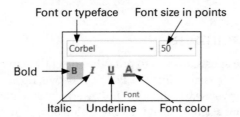

Change Basic Character Formatting

All four Office Online apps (Word, Excel, PowerPoint, and OneNote) have a Font group (called Basic Text in OneNote) with at least six settings: font, font size, font color, bold, italic, and underline, as shown in Figure 3-8. Many of the apps have additional text formatting settings that will be discussed in the chapters on the particular app.

Office Online provides a number of options for the font and font size as shown next in Word. Click the down arrows to select a font or font size. You can also type a size in the text box.

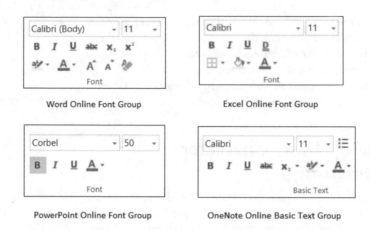

Word Online Font Group   Excel Online Font Group

PowerPoint Online Font Group   OneNote Online Basic Text Group

FIGURE 3-8   Office Online provides a consistent set of text formatting options in all apps.

Print a Document

All Office Online apps allow you to print the currently active contents of an app. In all cases, click the File tab and click Print. The Print option will open, as shown next for Word. An image will open to show you what will print. In PowerPoint, the image is in PDF (Adobe Acrobat) format. Click Print again to open the Print dialog box, shown in Figure 3-9, again for Word. Here you can select the local printer you want to use, the number of copies, the pages, size, and orientation you want. (In Excel, click Print three times, and the only option is whether you're printing all or a selected part of the worksheet.)

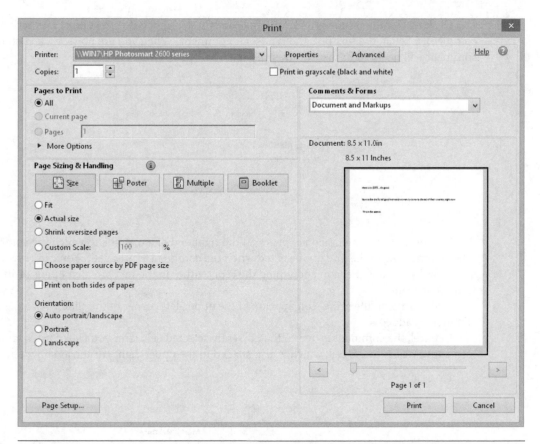

FIGURE 3-9   The Print dialog box that opens with Office Online apps is different in each app.

    If you want to save a PowerPoint PDF image, press ALT on your keyboard and choose File | Save As, select the location and name for saving the image, and click Save.

Enter Comments

Three of the Office Online apps enable you to insert comments using the same option on the Insert ribbon.

Clicking Comment opens a Comments pane on the right with a text box for entering a comment. Click in the text box and type your comment. When you are done, click Post. The comment will be listed in the Comments pane.

In Word, the comment icon appears on the right end of a text line to which the comment refers (something in the line was selected when the comment was added). You can reply to a comment by clicking the icon and typing the reply, either in the text box that opens or in the Comments pane.

In PowerPoint, the same icon appears in the upper-left corner of the slide where a comment is added.

In Excel, the comment is tied to the currently selected cell; after you click Post, a comment icon appears next to the cell, which is also shaded in the upper-right corner, as shown next:

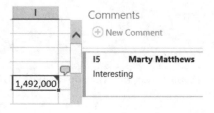

4

Working with Word Online

HOW TO...

- Create a new Word Online document
- Use a template to create a document
- Locate and open an existing document
- Work with text
- Navigate in a document
- Use Word writing aids

Using Word Online, you can create and edit *documents*, such as letters, reports, invoices, scripts, and books. Documents come in many forms, from the hardback printed book, to e-books on tablets and headlines on smart phones. In fact, this book was written in Word. You may be viewing it in book form or on a tablet.

In the computer, a document is a called a *file*, an object that has been given a name and is stored on the hard drive. For example, the name given to the Word file for this chapter is Chap04.docx. "Chap04" is the filename, and ".docx" is the file extension. By default, documents saved in Word Online are saved with the .docx extension.

In this chapter you'll briefly review from earlier chapters how to create new documents and find existing ones. Then you'll see how to enter, change, and delete text; find and replace text; and select, copy, and move text. You'll also learn how to use some special tools, such as highlighting.

Explore Word Online

If you are already accustomed to working with Word on the desktop, this section will serve as a review. If you are not acquainted with Word, this section will introduce you to the important terms and concepts you need to understand to work with Word Online. Then it will give you a brief look at the different views you can use when creating a document and introduce you to other important concepts and tools you'll find in Word Online.

From here on we'll use just "Word" to refer to "Word Online" unless it is necessary to distinguish what is being discussed. If we need to refer to the version installed on your computer, we'll use "Word desktop," which will include any version of Word that is installed on any device and not online.

Start Word

As you learned in Chapter 3, you start Word by opening a browser, typing **office.com**, pressing ENTER, and clicking the Word Online icon.

Alternatively, in the browser window, type **onedrive.com**, sign in if asked, click the down arrow to the right of OneDrive, and click the Word Online icon to open Word.

When you first open Word, you'll see the Let's Get Started banner. From here, you can open a new blank document, browse templates, or open recent documents on OneDrive. We'll look at all three options in this chapter.

 To bypass the Let's Get Started banner when you start Word, open an existing document by opening OneDrive and clicking a Word document. Word will open and display the document.

Create a New Document

Click New Blank Document. Word will open with a blank document into which you can start typing immediately, as you can see in Figure 4-1.

The blinking bar in the upper-left corner of the document pane, called the *insertion point*, indicates where the text you type will appear. Also, the mouse pointer becomes an I-beam that will fit between characters on the screen.

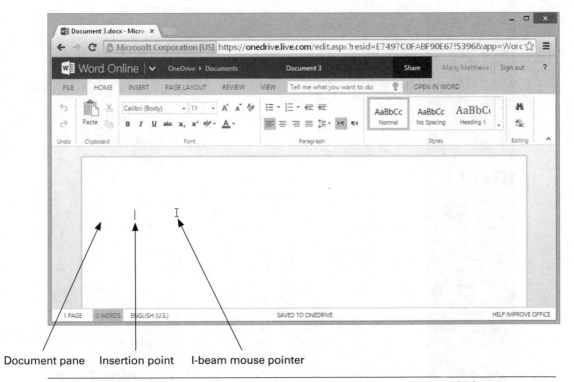

Document pane   Insertion point   I-beam mouse pointer

FIGURE 4-1   When you first start Word, the blank document pane is ready for you to create a document immediately.

Your ribbon options will vary depending on the size of the window. Windows that are not maximized in size display abbreviated options, such as the Styles and Editing groups on the right end of the ribbon, shown next.

Use a Template to Create a Document

To use a template to create a document, click Browse Templates in the Let's Get Started banner, or, with Word open, do the following:

1. Click the File tab, and then click New. The New screen will open, as shown in Figure 4-2, displaying several templates you can use, an option to create a blank document, and a link you can click to get more templates on Office.com.

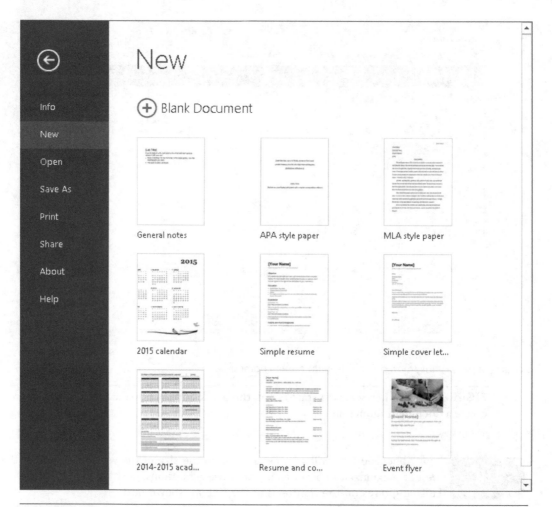

FIGURE 4-2 The New screen gives you a number of templates for starting a document.

2. Review the templates that are displayed. If you find one you like, click it. If you don't see a template that will work for you, click More On Office.com. The Office online template page will open, as shown in Figure 4-3. This is the same page that opens when you click Browse Templates in the Let's Get Started banner.

3. Scroll through the templates. If you still do not see what you want, click one or more categories in the list on the left and review the templates that are displayed.
    Make sure you look carefully at the template choices. Some of these templates are for Word documents, but not all of them.

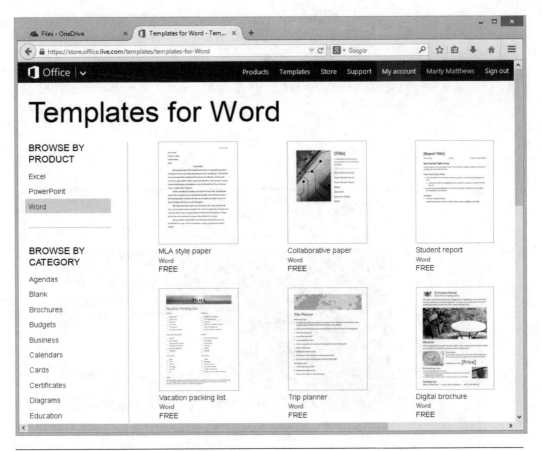

FIGURE 4-3 Office.com adds many more templates for you to choose from.

4. When you find the right template, click it. A preview page will open with more options.
5. If you want to use a template from Office.com, click Open In Word Online. The template will be saved to your OneDrive. Click Continue and a document with the selected template opens, as you can see in Figure 4-4.

Locate and Open an Existing Document

After you create, save, and close a document, you may want to reopen it later, either to read it or to make further revisions. Similarly, you may want to open a Word document created by someone else, or open a document created in another word processing program. In any case, you must first locate the document and then open it in Word. You can locate the document either directly from Word if it is in OneDrive or by searching for it using OneDrive's Upload feature and then placing it in a folder on OneDrive.

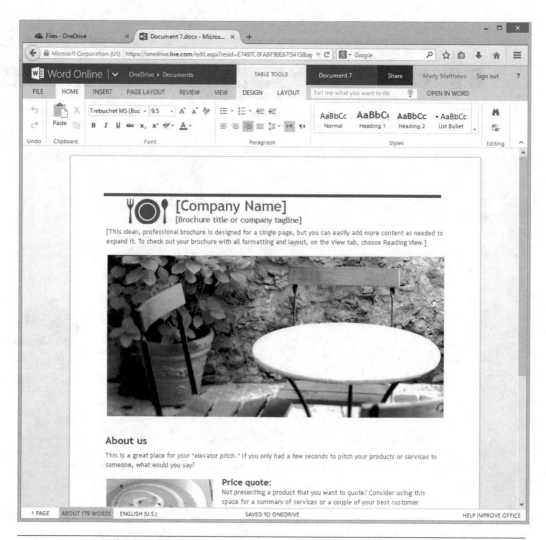

FIGURE 4-4 Templates provide not only a layout, but also a number of ideas for content.

 To return to the Word window from the File menu screen, click the left-pointing arrow in the upper-left corner of the page.

To locate, upload, and open a document, follow these steps:

1. Open OneDrive, open the folder in which you want to upload the document or file (document and file are synonymous here), click Upload, and navigate through the disks, folders, and files to which you have access to locate the file you want.

2. Double-click the file you want (or hold down CTRL while clicking several files and then click Open) to upload the file (or files) to the OneDrive folder.

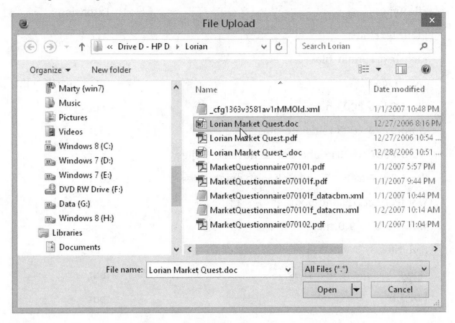

3. In the folder that contains the file, click the file to open it in Word.
4. When you open an existing document in Word, it is in Word Online where you can perform many of the Word functions. In this book we assume you are using Word Online. However, if you have Word installed on your computer, you can choose to edit the document in Word on your computer.

If you want to open and edit a word-processing document created in a program other than Word, you can most likely open it and edit it in Word. Table 4-1 shows the file types Word can open.

As good as Word's automatic saving feature is, it is a great idea to save your document manually at least a couple of times per hour as you work. Doing this can save you the frustration of working several hours on a document only to lose it. Chapter 3 shows you how to save a document.

TABLE 4-1 File Types That Word Can Open Directly

File Type	Extension
Plain text files	.txt
Rich Text Format files	.rtf
Web page files	.htm, .html, .mht, .mhtml
Word 97 to 2003 files	.doc
Word 97 to 2003 template files	.dot
Word 2007 to 2013 and Online document files	.docx
Word 2007 to 2013 and Online template files	.dotx
WordPerfect 5.x and 6.x files	.doc, .wpd
Works 6.0 to 9.0 files	.wps
XML files	.xml
Open Document Text files	.odt
PDF files	.pdf

Write a Document

Whether you create a new document or open an existing one, you will likely want to enter and edit text. Editing, in this case, includes adding and deleting text as well as selecting, moving, and copying it.

Enter Text

To enter text in a document that you have newly created or opened, simply start typing. The characters you type will appear in the document pane at the insertion point (the blinking vertical bar shown in Figure 4-1) and in the order in which you type them.

Determine Where Text Will Appear

The location of the insertion point determines where text that you type will appear. In a new document, the insertion point is located in the upper-left corner of the document pane and remains there until you enter text. It is also placed there by default when you open an existing document. When you enter text, the insertion point moves, or is pushed, to the right, and stays to the right of the last character you typed. However, you can move the insertion point within or to the end of existing text using either the keyboard or the mouse.

New text pushes the insertion point to the right

Move the Insertion Point with the Keyboard

When Word is open and a document is active, the insertion point moves every time you press a character or directional key on the keyboard (unless a menu or dialog box is open). The directional keys are TAB, BACKSPACE, and ENTER; the four arrow keys; and HOME, END, PAGE UP, and PAGE DOWN.

Move the Insertion Point with the Mouse

When the mouse pointer is in the document pane, it appears as an I-beam, as you saw in Figure 4-1. The I-beam shape is used because it fits between characters on the screen. You can move the insertion point by moving the I-beam mouse pointer to where you want the insertion point and then clicking the mouse.

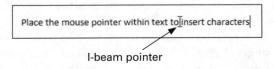

Place the mouse pointer within text to insert characters

I-beam pointer

Insert Text or Type Over It

When you press a letter, symbol, or number key with Word in its default mode (as it is when you first start it), the insertion point and any existing text to the right of the insertion point is pushed to the right and down on a page. This is also true when you press the TAB or ENTER key. This is called *insert* mode. There is also *overtype* mode that can be turned on by pressing the INSERT key but is now turned off by default, so pressing the INSERT key now does nothing. You must first select the text to be overtyped before you type over it.

Insert Line or Page Breaks

In Word, you simply keep typing and the text will automatically wrap around to the next line. You manually intervene only when you want to break a line before it would otherwise end. Manual line breaks are used in three instances:

- To start a new paragraph, press ENTER. When you break a line this way, you can format the new paragraph differently.
- To start a new line, press SHIFT-ENTER. This new line is considered part of the previous paragraph and retains its formatting.
- To force the start of a new page, press CTRL-ENTER. You may want to start a new page, for instance, at the end of the last paragraph in a part of the document, so that you can start a new part and paragraph on a new page.

You can also enter a page break using the mouse. With the insertion point positioned where you want the break to occur, click the Insert tab, and click Page Break in the Pages group. A page break will be inserted in the text. (If your screen is small-sized, you'll have to click Pages and select the option from the menu.)

Select Text

To copy, move, delete, or overtype text, you first need to select it. When you *select text,* you identify it as a separate block from the rest of the text in a document. You can select text with either the mouse or the keyboard. You can select any amount of text, from a single character to an entire document. As you select the text, it is highlighted with a colored background, as you can see in Figure 4-5, and a mini toolbar for character editing is displayed.

Select Text with the Mouse

You can select varying amounts of text with the mouse.

- **Select a single character** or any amount of text by dragging over it:
  1. Move the mouse pointer to the right or left of the first character.
  2. Press and hold the mouse button while dragging the mouse pointer to the left or right of the last character. The selected text will be highlighted.
- **Select a single character** or any amount of text, by clicking:
  1. Click to place the insertion point to the left of the first character.
  2. Press and hold SHIFT while dragging the mouse or clicking to the right of the last character or word you want to select. The selected range of text will be highlighted.
- **Select a single word** by double-clicking it.
- **Select a single paragraph** by rapidly clicking three times in the paragraph.

 After selecting one area using the keyboard, the mouse, or both, you can select further independent areas by pressing and holding CTRL while using any of the mouse selection techniques.

The Gettysburg Address

Gettysburg, Pennsylvania
November 19, 1863
Abraham Lincoln

Four score and seven years ago our fathers brought forth [Century Gothic ▾ 12 ▾ A˄ A˅ A▴ Styles] nation, conceived in Liberty, and dedicated to the propo [B I U ab▾ A▾ ☰▾ ☷▾] equal. Now we are engaged in a great civil war, testing whether that nation or any nation so conceived and so dedicated, can long endure. We are met on a great battle-field of that war. We have come to dedicate a portion of that field, as a final resting place for those who here gave their lives that that nation might live. It is altogether fitting and proper that we should do this.

But, in a larger sense, we can not dedicate -- we can not consecrate -- we can not hallow -- this ground. The brave men, living and dead, who struggled here, have consecrated it, far above our poor power to add or detract. The world will little note, nor long

---

FIGURE 4-5 You will always know exactly what text you are moving, copying, or deleting because it is highlighted on the screen.

Select Text with the Keyboard

You can also select varying amounts of text using only the keyboard.

- To **select a single character** or any amount of text, use the arrow keys to move the insertion point to the right or left of the first character you want to select, and then press and hold SHIFT while using the arrow keys to move the insertion point to the left or right of the last character.
- To **select an entire line of text**, place the insertion point at the beginning of the line by pressing HOME, and then press SHIFT-END.
- To **select an entire document**, press CTRL-A.

 You select a picture by clicking it. Once selected, a picture can be copied, moved, or deleted from a document in the same ways as text, using the Clipboard. (See Chapter 3 for more details about the Clipboard.)

Copy and Move Text

Copying and moving text are similar actions. Think of copying text as moving it and leaving a copy behind. You can copy or move text in two steps:

1. Selected text is copied or cut (removed) from its current location and placed automatically on the Clipboard.
2. The contents of the Clipboard are pasted to a new location, as identified by the insertion point.

 The Office Clipboard is shared by all Office products. You can copy or cut objects and text from any Office application, which automatically saves it to the Clipboard. Then it is available to paste into the same or one or more other Office applications. Refer to Chapter 3 to find out more about the Office Clipboard.

Cut Text

When you *cut* text, you place it on the Clipboard and delete it from its current location. After you paste the text from the Clipboard to a new location, the text has been *moved* and no longer exists in its original location. To cut and place text on the Clipboard, select it and then use one of these techniques:

- Press CTRL-X.
- Right-click the text and choose Cut from the context menu.
- In the Home tab Clipboard group, click Cut.

Depending on your browser, you may be asked whether you want to allow this web page to access your Clipboard. Under normal circumstances you can click Allow Access. Alternatively, you may be told that your browser does not allow access to your Clipboard.

Copy Text

When you *copy* text to the Clipboard, you also leave it in its original location. After you paste the text from the Clipboard to a new location in the document, the same text will appear in two places in the document: at the original location and at the pasted location. To copy text to the Clipboard, select it and then use one of these techniques:

- Press CTRL-C.
- Right-click the text and click Copy from the context menu.
- In the Home tab Clipboard group, click Copy.

Paste Text

To complete a copy or a move, you must *paste* the text from the Clipboard either to the same or to another document where the insertion point is located. A copy of the text stays on the Clipboard and can be pasted again. To paste the contents of the Clipboard at the insertion point, do one of the following:

- Press CTRL-V.
- Right-click and choose Paste from the context menu.
- In the Home tab Clipboard group, click Paste.

Undo a Move or Paste Action

You can undo a move or paste action with one of these techniques:

- Press CTRL-Z.
- In the Home tab Undo group, click Undo.

Redo an Undo Action

You can redo many undo actions, which restores the action previously cancelled, with one of these techniques:

- Press CTRL-Y.
- In the Home tab Undo group, click Redo.

Delete Text

Deleting text removes it from its current location *without* putting it on the Clipboard. To delete selected text, press DELETE (or DEL).

 You can recover deleted text by clicking Undo in the Home tab Undo group.

Enter Symbols and Special Characters

Entering a keyboard character into your document takes only a keystroke, but many other characters and symbols exist beyond those that appear on the keyboard (for example, ©, £, Ã, Ω, ʌɔ, and •). You can enter these characters and symbols using a sequence of keys (also called a *keyboard shortcut*) that must be entered on the numeric keypad. The following steps show how that is done:

1. Move the insertion point where you want to insert the symbol or special character.
2. Press NUM LOCK to put the numeric keypad into numeric mode.
3. Press and hold ALT while pressing all four digits (including the leading zero) on the numeric keypad, not the regular numeric keys above the keypad. The special character digits are shown in Table 4-2.
4. Release ALT. The symbol or special character is inserted where the insertion point is located.

The shortcut keys for some of the more common special characters are shown in Table 4-2 and look like this when they are inserted in a Word document:

TABLE 4-2   **Shortcut Keys for Special Characters**

Character	Name	Shortcut Keys
•	Bullet	ALT-0149
©	Copyright	ALT-0169
™	Trademark	ALT-0153
®	Registered	ALT-0174
£	Pound	ALT-0163
€	Euro	ALT-0128
…	Horizontal ellipsis	ALT-0133
–	En dash	ALT-0150
—	Em dash	ALT-0151

Navigate a Document

Understanding how to navigate a document is essential to your being able to work with it. *Navigating* in this context refers both to moving around in a document and to finding the text you need (and perhaps replacing it with something else).

Move Around in a Document

Word provides a number of ways to move around in a document using the mouse and the keyboard.

Use the Mouse and Scroll Bars

There are two scroll bars: one for moving vertically within the document, and one for moving horizontally. They are displayed only when your text is too wide or too long to fit completely on the screen. Each scroll bar contains four controls for getting you where you want to go. Using the vertical scroll bar, shown in Figure 4-6, you can do the following:

- **Move upward one line** by clicking the upward-pointing *scroll arrow*.
- **Move upward or downward** by dragging the *scroll button* in the corresponding direction.
- **Move up or down the screen's height** by clicking in the *scroll bar* above the scroll button to move toward the beginning of the document, or below the scroll button to move toward the end of the document.
- **Move downward one line** by clicking the downward-pointing *scroll arrow*.

The horizontal scroll bar has similar controls, except they are used to move horizontally on the screen.

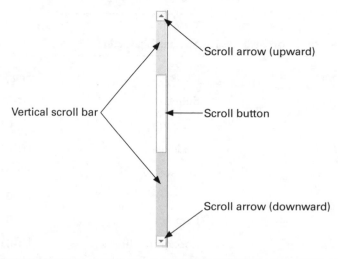

FIGURE 4-6 The vertical scroll bar and its button and arrows enable you to move easily to different locations within your document.

Move with the Keyboard

Use the following keyboard commands to move around a document and move the insertion point at the same time:

- Move left or right one character by pressing the LEFT or RIGHT ARROW key.
- Move up or down one line by pressing the UP or DOWN ARROW key.
- Move left or right one word by pressing CTRL-LEFT ARROW or CTRL-RIGHT ARROW.
- Move up or down one paragraph by pressing CTRL-UP ARROW or CTRL-DOWN ARROW.
- Move to the beginning or end of a line by pressing HOME or END.
- Move to the beginning or end of a document by pressing CTRL-HOME or CTRL-END.
- Move up or down one screen by pressing PAGE UP or PAGE DOWN.

Go to a Particular Location

You can go to a particular location in a document using the Go To command, by pressing CTRL-G, which opens the Search dialog box, as shown in Figure 4-7. Here you can enter a word or phrase, which takes you to the first occurrence of that word or phrase, and then, if you want, to following occurrences.

After opening the Search box, which displays the first word or phrase occurrence, click the down arrow in the Search box to go to the second occurrence, and so on.

Find and Replace Text

Often, you'll want to find particular text in a document, but you may not know where, or even how many times, that text occurs. This is especially true when you want to locate names or words that are sprinkled throughout a document. For example, if you had repeatedly referred

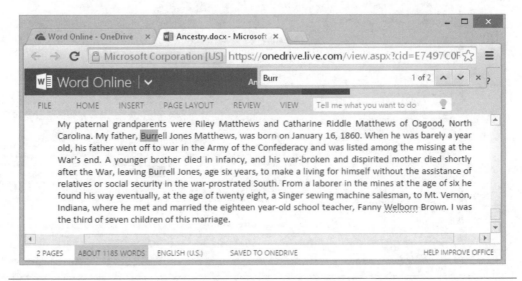

FIGURE 4-7   The Go To command allows you to search for a particular word or phrase within a document.

to a table on page 4 and the table was subsequently moved to page 5, you would need to search for all occurrences of "page 4" and change them to "page 5." In this example, you not only want to *find* "page 4," but also want to *replace* it with "page 5."

In addition to enabling you to do a simple search for a word or phrase, as in the previous example, Word enables you to search for parts of words and to match the case to search for a particular capitalization.

Find Text

Find allows you to search for a word or phrase:

1. In the Home tab Editing group, click Find. The Find pane opens.
2. In the Find text box, type the word or phrase you want to find. As you type, the results are displayed in the lower part of the pane with the first result selected, as shown in Figure 4-8.
3. Click an individual search result in the Find pane and the document will be repositioned at that specific location so that you can see the search result in the document.
4. If you want your search to find a word that is also contained in another word, such as finding the word "ton" and not words like "Washington" or "tonic," click the down arrow at the right of the Find text box and click Find Whole Words Only.

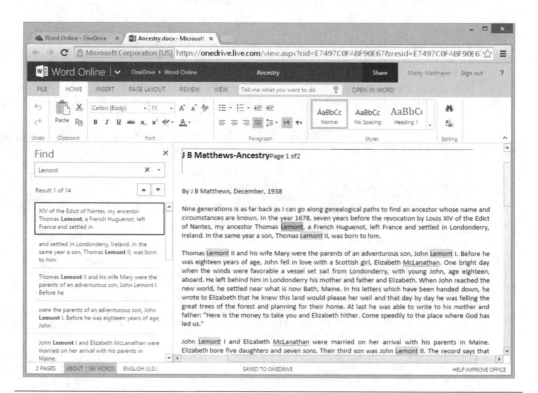

FIGURE 4-8 When you search for a word or phrase, the Find pane displays a list of results beneath the search criteria.

5. If you want to find a specific capitalization of a word or phrase, such as "OneNote" but not "onenote," click the down arrow at the right of the Find text box and click Match Case.

6. If you can't see all of the found results, or you want to move to another instance, use the up and down arrows at the top of the results.

7. When you are done, click Close in the upper-right corner of the Find pane.

Find and Replace Text

Often, the purpose of searching for a word, phrase, or other text is to replace it with something else. Word lets you use the features of Find to search for what you want and then replace what is found.

1. In the Home tab Editing group, click Replace. The Find And Replace pane appears, as shown in Figure 4-9.

2. In the Find text box, type the word or phrase you want to find. As you type, the results are displayed in the lower part of the pane with the first result selected.

3. In the Replace With text box, type the text with which you want to replace the found item(s).

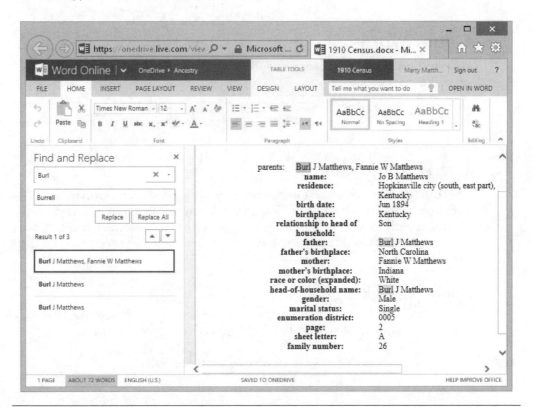

FIGURE 4-9   You can replace a single instance of text or replace all instances at once.

4. Choose one of the following options:
   - Click Replace if you want to replace the current instance with the text you entered in the Replace With text box. Word replaces this instance and automatically selects the next instance.
   - Click Replace All if you want to replace all occurrences of the text with the text you entered in the Replace With text box. Word replaces all instances at one time.
5. If you can't see all of the found results, or you want to move to another instance without replacing the selected one, use the up and down arrows at the top of the results.
6. When you are done, click Close in the upper-right corner of the Find And Replace pane.

 You can generally undo the last several operations by repeatedly issuing one of the Undo commands. If you accidentally click Replace All instead of Replace, clicking Undo once will undo all changes.

Use Word Writing Aids

Word provides several aids that can assist you not only in creating your document but also in making sure that it is as professional-looking as possible. These include word counts and highlighting.

Count Words

Word tells you the number of pages and words in a document in the status bar in the bottom-left of the window.

Use Highlighting

The Highlight feature is useful for marking important text in a document or text that you want to call a reader's attention to. Keep in mind, however, that highlighting parts of a document works best when the document is viewed on your screen or online. When printed, the highlighting marks often appear gray and may even obscure the text you're trying to call attention to.

Apply Highlighting

You click the Highlight button to apply a color highlighting to selected text. First you choose the text you want to highlight, and then choose a color to apply to the text.

1. Drag mouse pointer over the text you want to highlight.

2. In the Home tab Font group, click the Highlight icon, and select a color from the menu. The highlighting is applied to your selection.

> **The unanimous Declaration of the thirteen united States of America,**
>
> When in the Course of human events, it becomes necessary for one people to dissolve the
>
> political bands which have connected them with another, and to assume among the powers of the

Remove Highlighting

You can remove the highlighting from any highlighted text:

1. Select the text from which you want to remove highlighting, or press CTRL-A to select all of the text in the document.
2. In the Home tab Font group, click the Highlight icon, and then click No Color.

Change Highlighting Color

You can also change the color of the highlight:

1. Select the highlighted text for which you want to change the color of the highlight.
2. In the Home tab Font group, click the Highlight icon, and click the color that you want to use.

5

Formatting a Document

HOW TO...

- Format texts
- Select fonts and font styles
- Format paragraphs
- Set line spacing
- Set page margins, paper orientation, and paper size
- Use styles
- Add headers and footers
- Create and format tables

Plain, unformatted text conveys information, but not nearly as effectively as well-formatted text, as you can see by the two examples in Figure 5-1. Word provides numerous ways to format your text. Most fall under the categories of text formatting, paragraph formatting, and page formatting, which are discussed in the following sections of this chapter.

This chapter will discuss both the direct, or manual, application of formatting and the use of styles to apply formatting. Much of the character and paragraph formatting is commonly applied using styles that combine a number of individual formatting steps, saving you significant time over direct formatting. Direct formatting is usually applied only to a small amount of text that that is formatted differently from its style. The chapter will also discuss other formatting elements such as line spacing, paper size, and margins, as well as the use of tabs and the addition of headers and footers, footnotes and endnotes, and tables.

Format Text

You apply text formatting to individual characters, including the selection of fonts, font size, color, character spacing, and capitalization.

 Prior to applying formatting, you must select the text to be formatted. Chapter 4 contains an extensive section on selecting text.

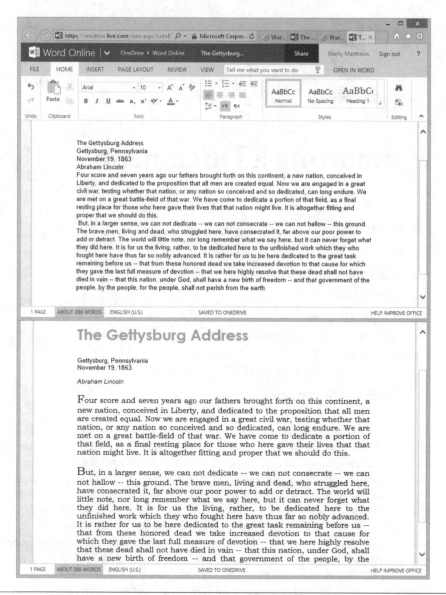

FIGURE 5-1 Formatting makes text both more readable and more pleasing to the eye.

Review the Text-Formatting Tools

To format text, you'll use keyboard shortcuts, the Font group on the Home tab, and the mini toolbar that displays when you select the text.

Use Keyboard Shortcuts

Using keyboard shortcuts to format text allows you to keep your hands on the keyboard. Table 5-1 summarizes the keyboard shortcuts for formatting text.

TABLE 5-1   Text-Formatting Shortcut Keys

Apply Formatting	Shortcut Keys
Align left	CTRL-L
Align right	CTRL-R
Bold	CTRL-B
Center	CTRL-E
Italic	CTRL-I
Underline	CTRL-U

Use the Font Group

You'll find that for most of your text formatting, you'll simply use the Font group (see Figure 5-2). To display the Font group tools, click the Home tab.

Use the Mini Toolbar

The mini toolbar is displayed automatically when you select text. You can also see it when you right-click text, which also displays a context menu. Many of the toolbar's buttons are also available in the Home tab's Font group. The mini toolbar also has buttons you click to create bulleted and numbered lists and to open the Styles menu. These buttons, along with the context menu, are described in this chapter.

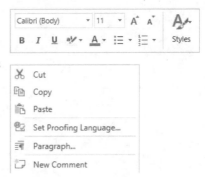

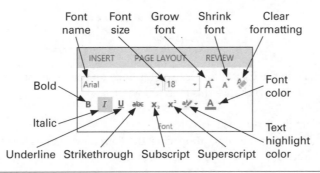

FIGURE 5-2   The Font group on the Home tab enables you to format quickly with the mouse.

Apply Character Formatting

Apply character formatting by selecting text and then applying a characteristic to it. For instance, you can apply a font, change the font size, make text bold or italic, underline it, or change the text color. You can format characters from the Home tab Font group, the mini toolbar that appears when you select text, or, in a few cases, with keyboard shortcuts.

Select a Font

A *font* is a set of characters that share a particular design, which is called a *typeface*. A number of fonts are available in Word. You can see the available fonts by clicking the down arrow next to the font name in the Home tab Font group (shown next) and then scrolling through the list (theme fonts are shown first, then your most recently used fonts, followed by all fonts listed alphabetically). You can see what each font looks like in the font list.

By default, the Calibri font is used for body text and Cambria is used for headings in all new documents. To change this font, follow these steps:

1. Select the text to be formatted.
2. In the Home tab Font group, click the Font down arrow. Scroll through the list until you see the font you want and then click it.

Several font types are included in the default set that is available in Word. Alphabetic fonts come in two varieties: *serif* fonts, such as Times New Roman or Century Schoolbook, for which each letter is designed with distinctive ends, or serifs, that appear as tiny lines stemming from and at an angle to the ends of a character's stroke, and *sans serif* ("without serifs") fonts, such as Arial and Century Gothic, without the attached lines. Sans-serif fonts are generally used for headings and lists, while serif fonts are generally used for body text in printed documents, but often the reverse is true in web pages.

Apply Bold or Italic Style

Fonts come in four styles: regular (or "Roman"), bold, italic, and bold-italic. The default is, of course, regular, yet fonts such as Arial Black appear bold. To make fonts bold, italic, or bold-italic, follow these steps:

1. Select the text to be formatted.
2. Press CTRL-B to make it bold, and/or press CTRL-I to make it italic. Alternatively, click the Bold and/or Italic icon in the Font group.

Change Font Size

Font size is measured in *points*, which is the height of a character, not its width. There are 72 points in an inch. For most fonts, the width varies with the character, the letter "i" taking up less room than "w," for example. (The Courier New font is an exception, with all characters having the same width.) The default font size is 11 points for body text, with standard headings varying from 11 to 14 points. The 8-point type is common for smaller print; anything below 6-point is typically unreadable. To change the font size of your text, do this:

1. Select the text to be formatted.
2. In the Home tab Font group, click the Font Size down arrow, and then click the font size you want from the list.

 At the top of the Font Size list, you can type in half-point sizes, such as 10.5, as well as sizes that are not on the list, such as 15.

Underline Text

Select the text to be formatted and use one of these options for underlining it:

- In the Home tab Font group, click the Underline icon.
- Press CTRL-U to apply a continuous underline to the entire selection (including spaces).

Change Font Color

To change the color of the text, follow these steps:

1. Select the text to be formatted.
2. In the Home tab Font group, click the Font Color button and choose a color from the drop-down menu.

Reset Text Formatting

Figure 5-3 shows some of the text formatting that has been or will be discussed.

All this formatting can be reset to the plain text or the default formatting. To reset text to default settings, follow these steps:

1. Select the text to be reset.
2. In the Home tab Font group, click the Clear Formatting button.

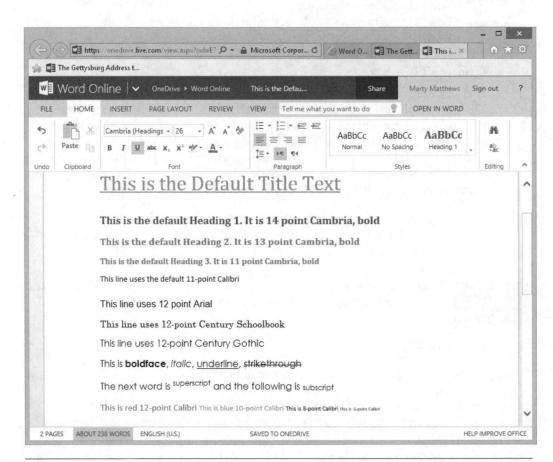

FIGURE 5-3 Character formatting must be applied judiciously, or it will detract from the appearance of a document.

Format a Paragraph

Apply *paragraph formatting* to any paragraph to manage alignment, indentation, line spacing, and bulleted or numbered lists. In Word, a paragraph ends with a paragraph mark (created by pressing ENTER) and contains any text or objects that appear between that paragraph mark and the previous paragraph mark. A paragraph can be empty, or it can contain anything from a single character to as many characters as you care to enter.

Survey the Paragraph-Formatting Tools

Paragraph formatting can be applied using the Paragraph dialog box, keyboard shortcuts, the Paragraph group on the Home tab, and the mini toolbar that displays when you select or right-click text (see "Use the Mini Toolbar" earlier in the chapter).

Access the Paragraph Dialog Box

The Paragraph dialog box provides a number of paragraph formatting and spacing alternatives. It can be opened in two ways:

- In the Home tab Paragraph group, click the down arrow to the right of the line spacing icon in the bottom-left corner. In the drop-down menu, click Line Spacing Options to open the Paragraph dialog box.
- Right-click the selected text you want to format and then click Paragraph in the lower context menu.

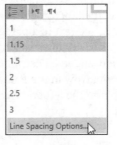

You can see that using the commands on the ribbon (Home tab Paragraph group) or the mini toolbar will be quicker and easier for most formatting tasks.

TABLE 5-2 Keyboard Shortcuts for Working with Paragraphs

Apply Formatting	Shortcut Keys
Left Align	CTRL-L
Right Align	CTRL-R
Center Align	CTRL-E
Justified	CTRL-J

Use Keyboard Shortcuts for Paragraphs

Use keyboard shortcuts to format paragraphs and keep your hands on the keyboard. Table 5-2 shows the keyboard shortcuts for formatting a paragraph.

Use the Paragraph Group

For most of your paragraph formatting, you'll simply use the Home tab Paragraph group (see Figure 5-4). To display the Paragraph group tools, click the Home tab. You can also open the Paragraph dialog box by right-clicking the paragraph you want to format and clicking Paragraph.

Set Paragraph Alignment

Four types of paragraph alignment are available in Word (see Figure 5-5): left aligned, centered, right aligned, and justified. Left aligned, right aligned, and centered are self-explanatory. *Justified* alignment means that the text in a paragraph is evenly spread between the left and right margins. Word does this by adding space between words, except for the last line of a paragraph, which is always left-aligned. Distributed alignment, an option available only when you click the Alignment down arrow in the Paragraph group, is similar to justified alignment in that it aligns the paragraph on the left and right, but it does this by adding space between characters instead of words.

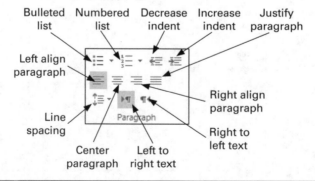

FIGURE 5-4 The Paragraph group in the Home tab contains many of the tools you need for formatting paragraphs.

Left Aligned
Four score and seven years ago our fathers brought forth on this continent a new nation dedicated to the proposition that all men are created equal. Now we are engaged in a great civil war, testing whether that nation, or any nation so conceived and so dedicated, can long endure.

Centered
Four score and seven years ago our fathers brought forth on this continent a new nation dedicated to the proposition that all men are created equal. Now we are engaged in a great civil war, testing whether that nation, or any nation so conceived and so dedicated, can long endure.

Right Aligned
Four score and seven years ago our fathers brought forth on this continent a new nation dedicated to the proposition that all men are created equal. Now we are engaged in a great civil war, testing whether that nation, or any nation so conceived and so dedicated, can long endure.

Justified
Four score and seven years ago our fathers brought forth on this continent a new nation dedicated to the proposition that all men are created equal. Now we are engaged in a great civil war, testing whether that nation, or any nation so conceived and so dedicated, can long endure.

Distributed
Four score and seven years ago our fathers brought forth on this continent a new nation dedicated to the proposition that all men are created equal. Now we are engaged in a great civil war, testing whether that nation, or any nation so conceived and so dedicated, can long endure.

FIGURE 5-5   Paragraph alignment provides both visual appeal and separation of text.

To apply paragraph alignment, click in the paragraph you want to align (you don't need to select the entire paragraph) and then choose one of the following options:

- In the Home tab Paragraph group, click the Align Text Left, Center, Align Text Right, or Justify button, depending on what you want to do.
- In the Home tab Paragraph group, click the Line Spacing down arrow and then click Line Spacing Options to open the Paragraph dialog box. Click the Alignment down arrow, click the type of alignment you want, and click OK. This is the only place where you can select distributed alignment.
- Use a keyboard shortcut. Refer to Table 5-2.

Indent a Paragraph

As illustrated in Figure 5-6, indenting a paragraph in Word means moving the left or right (or both) margins of the paragraph inward toward the center.

- An indented paragraph, either on the left or the right or on both the left and right, is used to separate and call attention to a piece of text.
- Indenting the first line of a paragraph is used to indicate the start of a new paragraph. In Word this can be done only by pressing TAB on the first line.
- Bulleted and numbered lists are used to organize and group pieces of text so they can be viewed as elements within a given topic.

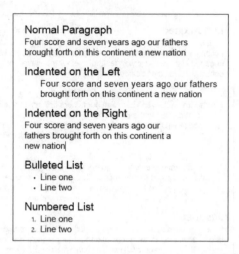

FIGURE 5-6 Indenting allows you to separate a block of text visually.

Change and Remove Indents

Indentation is a powerful formatting tool when used correctly. Like other formatting, it can also be overused and make text hard to read or to understand. Ask yourself two questions before you indent a paragraph: Do I have a good reason for it? Does it improve the readability and/or understanding of what is being said?

In all cases, unless otherwise noted, first click the paragraph for which you want to change or remove the indentation. Then do the following.

Increase or Decrease the Left Indent

To move the left edge of an entire paragraph to the right, or to move it back to the right, you have the following choices:

- In the Home tab Paragraph group, click Increase Indent one or more times to indent the left edge to the right a half-inch each time (the first click will move the left paragraph edge to the nearest half-inch or inch mark). To decrease the left indent, click Decrease Indent one or more times.
- In the Page Layout tab Paragraph group, under Indent, click the Left spinner's up arrow until you get the amount of indentation you want. To remove or reduce the indent, click the Left spinner's down-arrow.

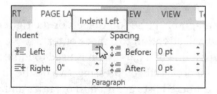

- Right-click the paragraph to be indented and click Paragraph to open the Paragraph dialog box. Under Indentation, click the Before Text spinner's up arrow until you get the amount of indentation you want, and then click OK. To reduce or remove the indentation, click the Before Text spinner's down-arrow.

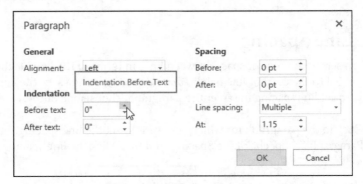

Increase or Decrease the Right Indent

To move the right edge of an entire paragraph to the left, you have these choices:

- In the Page Layout tab Paragraph group, under Indent, click the Right spinner's up arrow until you get the amount of indentation you want. To remove or reduce the right indent, click the Right spinner's down arrow.
- Right-click the paragraph to be indented and click Paragraph to open the Paragraph dialog box. Under Indentation, click the After Text spinner's up arrow until you get the amount of indentation you want, and then click OK. To reduce or remove the indentation, click the After Text spinner's down arrow.

Set Indents for Lists

To set the indents and options for a bulleted or numbered list, select the list and do one of the following:

- Click the down arrow opposite the bulleted or numbered list icon in the Home tab Paragraph group to select the type of bullets or numbering, and then use the Increase or Decrease indent in the same group.

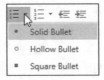

- Right-click the list to open the mini toolbar, and then click the down arrow opposite the bulleted or numbered list icon in the Home tab Paragraph group to select the type of bullets or numbering. Right-click the list again, click Paragraph, and use the Indentation spinners to adjust the indent.

Understand Line and Paragraph Spacing

The vertical spacing, or line spacing, of text is determined by the amount of space between lines, the amount of space added before and after a paragraph, and where line and page breaks occur.

Set Line Spacing

You can set the amount of space between lines in terms of the line height, with *single spacing* being equal to the current line height, *double spacing* being twice the current line height, and so on. To set line spacing for an entire paragraph, choose one of these options:

- Click in the paragraph for which you want to set the line spacing. In the Home tab Paragraph group, click Line Spacing, and then click the line spacing that you want to use.

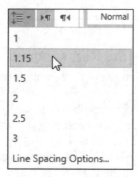

- Right-click the paragraph for which you want to set the line spacing. Click Paragraph, and click the Line Spacing down arrow. From the menu that appears, select the line spacing you want to use. Or click in the Line Spacing text box to open the At text box and use its spinners to set line spacing. Click OK.

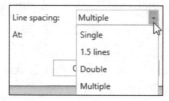

Add Space Between Paragraphs

In addition to specifying space between lines within paragraphs, you can add extra space before and after paragraphs. When typewriters were still in use, sometimes typists would add an extra blank line between paragraphs, which was often common in business letters. This has carried over to computers, but it does not always look good if you simply insert a blank line space. If you are using single spacing with 12-point type, for example, leaving a blank line will normally leave an extra 14 points between paragraphs. Common paragraph spacing equals 3 points before the paragraph and 6 points afterward, so if two of these paragraphs fell one after the other, a total of

9 points would appear between paragraphs, in comparison to the 14 points from an extra blank line. To add extra space between paragraphs, click the paragraph to which you want to add space, and then choose one of these options:

- In the Page Layout tab Paragraph group, under Spacing, click the Before and After spinners to set the spacing before and after the paragraph.

- Right-click the paragraph and click Paragraph. Under Spacing, click the Before spinner or enter a number in points ("pt") for the space you want to add before the paragraph. If desired, do the same thing for the space after the paragraph. Alternatively, click the spinners. Then click OK.

Set Line and Page Breaks

The vertical spacing of a document is also affected by how lines, paragraphs, and pages are broken or divided. You can break a line and start a new one, thereby creating a new line, a new paragraph, or a new page. Do the following:

- To create a new paragraph, move the insertion point to where you want to break the line and press ENTER.
- To advance to a new line while staying in the same paragraph, move the insertion point to where you want to break the line and press SHIFT-ENTER.
- To break a page and start a new one, move the insertion point to where you want to break the page and press CTRL-ENTER, or click Page Break on the Insert tab Pages group.

If you format a single paragraph the way you want a group of paragraphs to look, you can often just press ENTER to begin a new paragraph with the same formatting. This is, of course, mandatory with a line break, which must be the same as the preceding text. See "Use Styles," later in this chapter.

Format a Page

Page formatting has to do with the overall formatting of items, such as margins, orientation, size, and vertical alignment of a page. You can set options for page formatting either from the Page Layout tab or the Page Setup dialog box.

Set Margins

Margins are the space between the edge of the paper and the text. To set margins, follow these steps:

1. Open the document whose margins you want to set.
2. In the Page Layout tab Page Setup group, click Margins to open the menu shown in Figure 5-7.

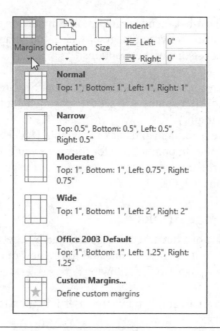

FIGURE 5-7   You can select from a group of predefined margins, according to the needs of your document, or you can create a custom set of margins.

3. Click the option you want. For any of the preset margins, they will be applied as shown.
4. If you select Custom Margins, the Margins dialog box opens. Change the margins you want, and click OK.

 Remember that page formatting changes the margins and other formatting for whole pages. To change margin formatting for smaller sections of text, use indenting.

Determine Page Orientation

Page orientation specifies whether a page is taller than it is wide (portrait) or wider than it is tall (landscape). For $8\frac{1}{2}$-inch by 11-inch letter size paper, if the 11-inch side is vertical (the left and right edges), which is the standard way of reading a letter, it is a portrait orientation. If the 11-inch side is horizontal (the top and bottom edges), it is a landscape orientation.

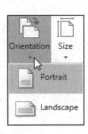

Portrait orientation is the default orientation in Word and most documents. To change it, follow these steps:

1. Open the document whose orientation you want to set.
2. In the Page Layout tab Page Setup group, click Orientation.
3. Click the option you want.

Specify Paper Size

Specifying the paper size gives you the starting perimeter of the area within which you can set margins and enter text or pictures.

1. In the Page Layout tab Page Setup group, click Size. A menu will open.

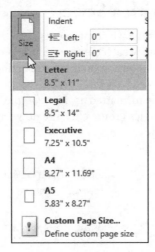

2. Click the size of paper you want. For any of the preset sizes, they will be applied as shown.
3. If you select Custom Page Size, the Page Size dialog box opens. Enter the width and height you want, and click OK.

Use Styles

Word provides a gallery of styles comprising sets of canned formatting choices, such as font, bold, and color, that you can apply to headings, titles, text, and lists. You use styles by identifying what kind of formatting a selected segment of text needs, such as for a header or title. Then, using the gallery of styles, select the style to apply to the selected text. Formatting will be applied smoothly and easily. You can easily change style sets and create new ones.

Note   Many of the tools in Word, such as the tool that creates a table of contents, are available only after the style of the text has been identified. For instance, you cannot create a table of contents if you have not identified which lines of text are headings and subheadings. By default, all text starts out with the Normal style.

Understand Styles

Using styles and templates, you can apply formatting to your documents quickly and easily to make them consistent and professional looking.

A *style* applies a specific set of formatting characteristics to individual characters or to entire paragraphs. For example, you can apply styles to headings, titles, lists, and other text components. Consequently, styles determine how the document's overall design comes together in its look and feel. Styles are beneficial to document creation, because they provide an integrated and consistent platform to all formatted text. You can change styles within a document, as desired.

You use a *template* to set up a document with a unique set of styles. Templates were discussed in Chapter 4.

Identify Text with a Style

Within your document you have components such as headings, titles, lists, regular paragraphs, and so on. You must identify each component for Word to know how to format these according to a given style. You can do this by selecting text and clicking the appropriate style.

1. Select the text to be formatted as, for example, a title or heading.
2. In the Home tab Styles group, click the down arrow in the lower-right corner. The Styles gallery is displayed.

AaBbCc	AaBbCc	AaBbCc	**AaBbC**	AaBbCc
Normal	No Spacing	Heading 1	Heading 2	Heading 3
AaBbCc	AaBbCc	AaBbCc	*AaBbCc*	AaBbCc
Heading 4	Heading 5	Heading 6	Heading 7	Heading 8
AaBbCc	AaB	AaBbCc	*AaBbCc*	*AaBbCc*
Heading 9	Title	Subtitle	Subtle Emp...	Emphasis
AaBbCc	**AaBbCc**	*AaBbCc*	*AaBbCc*	AaBbCc
Intense Em...	Strong	Quote	Intense Qu...	Subtle Refe...
AaBbCc	***AaBbCc***	AaBbCc		
Intense Ref...	Book Title	List Paragra...		

$\frac{A_4}{Z}$ Apply Styles...

A Clear Formatting

3. Click the style you want to assign to the selected text. For example, for a top-level heading, select your main heading text and then click Heading 1 in the Styles gallery.

To change a text style to another one, first select the text and then in the Home tab Styles group, click the down arrow at the lower-right and choose an alternative style from the Styles gallery.

Clear a Style from Text or a Document

When you clear or delete a style from text, the text is reformatted with the Normal style. To clear the formatting of a whole document or of certain text, perhaps because you have applied the wrong style or you don't like how it looks, use the following options.

Delete Style from Selected Text

Select the specific text that you want to clear of formatting. Then do one of the following:

- In the Home tab Font group, click Clear Formatting.
- In the Home tab Styles group, click the down arrow on the right and click Clear Formatting.
- Right-click the selected text, and in the mini toolbar, click Styles to open the Styles gallery, and then click Clear Formatting.

Work with Documents

In addition to using styles to format your documents, you can use tabs, headers and footers, and footnotes and endnotes to refine your documents.

Use Tabs

A *tab* is a type of formatting used to align text and create simple tables. By default, Word has preplaced *tab stops* (the horizontal positioning of the insertion point when you press TAB) every half-inch. Tabs are better than space characters to create constant positioning, because tabs are set to specific measurements, while spaces may not always align the way you intend due to the size and spacing of individual characters in a given font.

To align text with a tab, click to the left of the text that you want aligned and press the TAB key.

 Indents, in addition to tabs, are another way to set indentation for a paragraph or list. You have several alternatives for adjusting indents, depending on the type of text with which you're working. Indentation is explored earlier in this chapter.

Add Headers and Footers

Headers and footers are placed at the top or bottom, respectively, of a document and contain information such as page numbers, revision dates, and the document title. The header appears at the top of every page, and the footer appears at the bottom of every page.

Create a Header or Footer

The header and footer are each formatted as a three-section, single-row table (or maybe a three-section text box). The left section is left aligned, the middle section is centered, and the right section is right-aligned. You can create or edit a header or footer for an open document as follows:

1. In the Insert tab Header & Footer group, click Header & Footer. Tables for adding a header and footer are displayed without content, but with the Table Tools contextual ribbons shown in Figure 5-8 (the reason this is called a "table" and not a "text box."

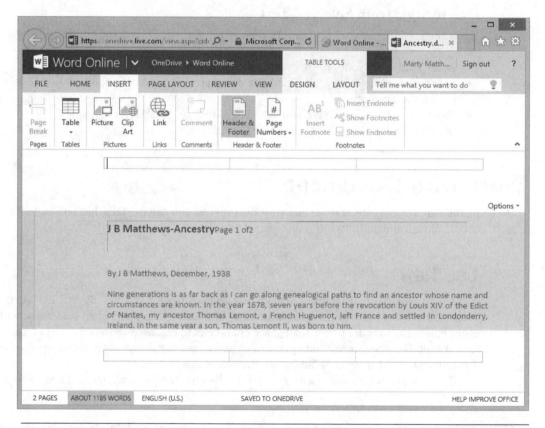

FIGURE 5-8 Headers and footers provide consistent information across the tops and bottoms of your document pages.

The Table Tools ribbons show that the header or footer is constructed as a table. Most of the tools in the Table Tools ribbons, however, are used only with normal tables and are not relevant to headers and footers.

2. The header and footer tables will automatically provide a left-aligned section, such as for a date; a centered middle section, for a title perhaps; and a right-aligned section, often for a page number. If you want an alignment different from the predefined alignment, click in the section and use the alignment options in the Table Tools Layout tab Alignment group.

3. To enter content, use the following steps as an example of how to proceed:
   a. Click in the first or left section to select it and type the date.
   b. Press TAB to move to the next (middle) section and type the title.
   c. Press TAB to go to the last (rightmost) section and, if desired, type **Page**. You'll see how to add a page number later in the "Insert Page Numbers" section.
   d. Format the text as desired using the Home tab.

January 14th, 2016	**Matthews Ancestry**	Page

4. When finished, click in the document area to close the header and footer tables.

Tip Once you close the header and footer area, the onscreen headers and footers are hidden. But you can redisplay them at any time by clicking the View tab Header & Footer button. The Insert tab Header & Footer button also redisplays the header and footer.

View and Edit a Header or Footer

Once you have a header and/or footer in a document, you can view them and edit them with these steps:

1. Open the header and footer tables by clicking Header & Footer in the Insert or View tab Header & Footer group. The header and footer tables will be displayed along with the Table Tools contextual ribbons, as shown earlier in Figure 5-8.
2. Edit the header or footer. For example, you might revise text, change the font, apply bold formatting, or add a date or time.
3. When finished, click in the document area.

Note When you edit a header or footer, Word automatically changes the header or footer on every page throughout the document, unless you have added different headers or footers in different sections of the document.

Insert Page Numbers

You can add automatic page numbering in any of the three sections of the header or footer. Once you have identified where a page number is to go (or accepted the initial default format), you insert the actual number as described here.

1. Click Page Numbers in the Insert tab Header & Footer group.

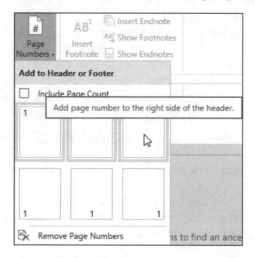

2. Click where you want the page number to appear. For the header example described earlier, you would click the upper-right box to add a page number on the right section.

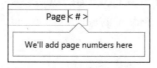

3. If you want to add a page count to the page number, click Include Page Count at the top of the Page Numbers group box.

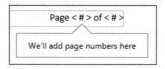

4. To remove a page number and its associated page count, if applicable, click Remove Page Numbers at the bottom of the Page Number group box.

 Notice that a blank space is automatically added to the left of the page number.

Apply Header and Footer Options

While the header and footer tables are displayed, you can open an Options menu to customize headers and footers.

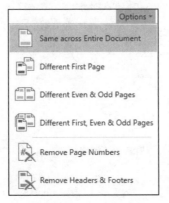

Use Multiple Headers and Footers

By default, a single header and footer is used throughout the document, but the Options menu enables you to choose a different set on the first page, different sets on odd and even pages, or a combination of the two. For example, you may not want to repeat the title header on the first page, or you may plan to bind the document, so you want the page number to show on the outer edge of each page—at the left on even-numbered pages and at the right on odd-numbered pages. Or you might want different titling to appear on different pages, such as a title in the header of all even-numbered pages and the section name or other information on all odd-numbered pages.

When you choose any of the multiple-page options, additional header and footer tables appear, where you can enter different headers and footers, as shown in Figure 5-9.

To create multiple headers and/or footers, follow these steps:

1. Open the header and footer tables by clicking Header & Footer in the Insert tab Header & Footer group.
2. Click Options on the far-right of the document area and choose the option that you want.
3. On the left you will see the titles for the option you have chosen—for example, First Page, Even Pages, and Odd Pages. Click the header or footer option to display the header and footer tables for that option. Fill out the tables as desired (see "Create a Header or Footer" earlier in this chapter).
4. Click any additional options and fill out the tables for those options.
5. When you are done with headers and footers for your document, click anywhere in the normal page text.

Remove Headers, Footers, and Page Numbers

To remove headers, footers, and/or page number use these steps:

1. With the header and footers displayed, click the Options drop-down list on the right.
2. Click Remove Headers & Footers to remove the entire header and footer.

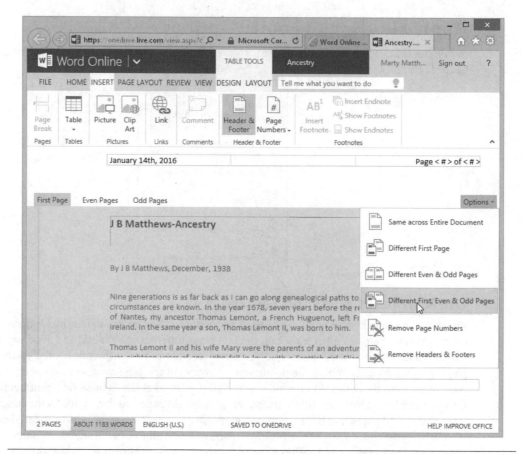

FIGURE 5-9 Word allows you to use up to three different headers and footers.

3. Word reminds you that all headers and footers and any page numbers will be removed. If that is OK, click Remove All.
4. To remove just the page numbering and leave the remainder of the headers and footers, click Remove Page Numbers.

If your document has multiple headers and footers, you must choose a different option to remove just one of your headers and footers. For example, if you have a different first page header and footer and you decide you want the same headers and footers to appear throughout the document, click Options | Same Across Entire Document to remove the first page header and footer.

Add Footnotes and Endnotes

Footnotes and *endnotes* are annotations within a document that provide reference citations or additional information for readers. The difference between the two is where they appear in a document. Footnotes appear either after the last line of text on the page or at the bottom of the page on which the annotated text appears. Endnotes appear either at the end of the section in which the annotated text appears or at the end of the document.

Insert a Footnote or Endnote

To add a footnote or endnote to a document, use the following steps:

1. Position the insertion point immediately after the text you want to annotate.
2. In the Insert tab Footnotes group, click Insert Footnote or Insert Endnote. For a footnote, the insertion point will be positioned at the bottom of the page; for an endnote, it will be positioned at the end of the document.

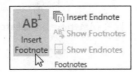

3. Type the text of the footnote or endnote, as shown in Figure 5-10.

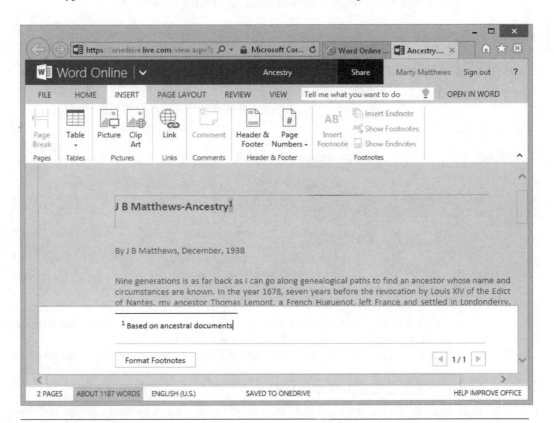

FIGURE 5-10   Footnotes and endnotes can be very useful for adding reference information you don't want in the body text.

4. If you want to reformat the footnote or endnote text, click Format Footnotes and apply the formatting you want.
5. When you're finished, click in the document to continue working in the text.

To see the text related to a footnote or an endnote after you have moved back to the body text, move the mouse to the footnote or endnote number and a bit of the note will appear; you can also open the note itself by clicking where indicated. Or you can click Show Footnotes or Show Endnotes in the Insert tab Footnotes group to see all the notes in the document.

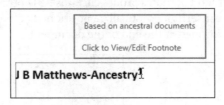

Change Footnotes or Endnotes

You can change an existing footnote or endnote with these steps:

1. Click Show Footnotes or Show Endnotes in the Insert tab Footnotes group.
2. Click in the note and make any changes.
3. Click Format Footnotes to open the Format Options dialog box. Make any changes to the font, font size, and indentation that you want, and then click Apply.

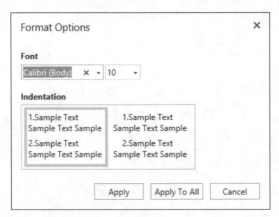

4. To move to the previous or the next note to make changes there, click the left or right arrow, respectively, in the lower-right corner.
5. When you are finished, click in the document to continue working in the text.

Delete a Footnote or Endnote

In the body of the document, select the number of the note you want to delete, and then press DELETE. Word automatically deletes the footnote or endnote and renumbers the notes.

When you delete an endnote or a footnote, be sure to delete the number in the annotation that appears in the document text. Word does not allow you to delete the note number and text in the footnote or endnote itself.

Use Tables

Use tables to divide information into rows and columns that create *cells* at their intersections. Tables can be used to arrange information systematically in rows and columns, or they can be used to lay out text and graphics in a document, as is done with headers and footers. Following are some of the ways that you can use tables:

- To display tabular data, with or without cell borders
- To create side-by-side columns of text
- To align labels and boxes for forms
- To separate and position text and accompanying graphics
- To place borders around text or graphics
- To place text on both sides of a graphic, or vice versa
- To add color to backgrounds, text, and graphics

Create a Table

When you create a table, you can specify the number of rows and columns to include. You can easily modify the table attributes after the original table is placed in your document. Follow these steps to create a table:

1. With the document open in Word, place the insertion point where you want the table to appear.
2. In the Insert tab Tables group, click Table to open the drop-down menu.
3. Each square in the menu represents one cell in your table. Click the cell that will appear at the lower-right corner of your table and all the cells in between will be highlighted. A table of that size will appear in the document at the location you indicated. In the following example, a three-column, three-row table is selected.

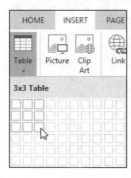

4. In each cell in the table, type in information, pressing TAB as needed to move from cell to cell.

Tip If you need a table that is larger than the 10 rows by 10 columns from the Table drop-down menu, start by creating a table of that size. Then you can add rows or columns to the table. See "Insert Rows and Columns" later in this chapter.

Modify Tables

Once you have created a table, you can work with two sets of tools to modify it: the table contextual tabs in the ribbon and the table contextual mini toolbar that opens when you right-click in a table.

Use the Table Contextual Tabs

When you create a table in Word, or select it after it has been created, the ribbon automatically displays two table-related tabs: Table Tools Design and Table Tools Layout.

In the Table Tools Layout tab, shown in Figure 5-11, you can modify a table in many ways, including selecting, deleting, and inserting various table elements, as well as aligning cell contents. In the Table Tools Design tab, shown later in the chapter in Figure 5-12, you can apply various styles to tables as well as add color and apply shading.

Both contextual tabs are discussed in "Work with Table Elements" and "Format Table Elements," later in this chapter.

Use the Table Contextual Mini Toolbar

Right-click a table or its contents and you'll see a contextual mini toolbar, where you can perform many of the formatting tasks available in the Home tab, as well as many of the table modification tasks in the Table Tools contextual tabs.

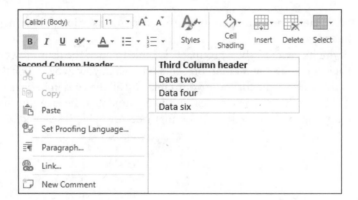

Work with Table Elements

Table elements include the table in total: its rows, columns, and cells. Word gives you the tools to select each of these elements so you can apply formatting or make other changes. It also provides tools to delete tables, rows, and columns, and to insert rows and columns, as you'll see in the next several sections.

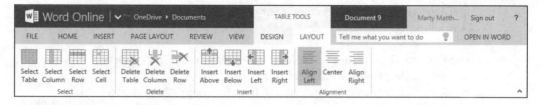

FIGURE 5-11   Use the Table Tools Layout tab to modify a table.

Select Tables, Rows, Columns, or Cells

Before you can perform many actions in a table, you must first select the element you are working with. You can do that by dragging, by using the Table Tools Layout tab, or via the table context mini toolbar. With the table open in Word, you can perform the following actions:

- To select an entire table, drag across the table from the upper-leftmost cell to the lower-rightmost cell. All the cells in the table will be highlighted, as shown.

First Column Header	Second Column Header	Third Column header
First Row header	Data one	Data two
Second Row header	Data three	Data four
Third Row header	Data five	Data six

- To select a row, drag across the row.
- To select a cell, drag across the contents of the cell. You cannot drag to select a column.
- To select a cell or a group of cells, click in the table where you want the selection to begin, and then in the Table Tools Layout tab Select group, click one of the following: Select Table, Select Column, Select Row, or Select Cell.

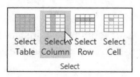

- To select a cell or a group of cells, right-click in the table where you want the selection to begin, and then in the context menu that opens, click Select and click one of the following: Select Table, Select Column, Select Row, or Select Cell.

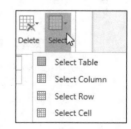

   You cannot drag to select a column.

Delete Tables, Rows, or Columns

You can make a table smaller by deleting rows and/or columns or you can delete a whole table. You can also delete contents of a cell, row, column, or table by selecting the contents and pressing DELETE. When you do that, the cell, row, column, or table itself remains in the document; only the contents are deleted.

To delete an entire table, column, or row and its contents, do one of the following:

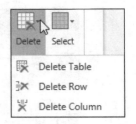

- Select the element, and in the Table Tools Layout tab, click Delete Table, Delete Column, or Delete Row.
- Right-click the table element, and in the mini toolbar that opens, click Delete, and then click Delete Table, Delete Row, or Delete Column.

Insert Rows and Columns

You can make a table larger by inserting a row or column on either side of a selected cell, row, or column. Do one of the following:

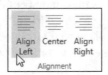

- Select a cell, row, or column, and in the Table Tools Layout tab, click Insert Above, Insert Below, Insert Left, or Insert Right.
- Right-click in a cell or a selected row or column and in the mini toolbar that opens, click Insert, and then click Insert Above, Insert Below, Insert Left, or Insert Right.

Align Contents in a Cell, Row, or Column

To align the contents in a cell, row, or column, select the element, and in the Table Tools Layout tab, click Align Left, Center, or Align Right.

Tip To insert a new line of regular text just before a table, click to the left of any contents in the top-leftmost cell and press ENTER.

Format Table Elements

Word provides several tools for formatting table elements in the Table Tools Design tab, shown in Figure 5-12. The first two groups, Table Styles Options and Table Styles, work together. The Table Style Options group adds accents to the styles. For example, the default selections shown in Figure 5-12 add accents to the header row and the first column, and provides for banded rows. The Table Styles are used to apply color and distinctive borders to a table's rows and columns. In the Change Colors menu, select the color used in the Table Styles. In the Cell Shading group, add color shading to any selected part of a table; this selection is completely separate from the rest of the Design tab. The best way to understand this is to try it out.

The best way to understand table design and style is to try it out. Let's do that.

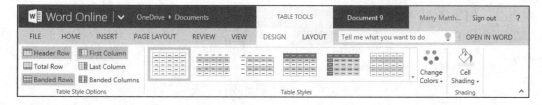

FIGURE 5-12   Use the Table Tools Design tab to apply styles and color to a table.

Apply Table Styles

If you use the default Design tab settings shown in Figure 5-12, you get a table that looks like the one shown next. The text in the header row and first column are bold, the borders are the selected blue, and a heavier border appears under the header row.

First Column Header	Second Column Header	Third Column header
First Row Header	Data one	Data two
Second Row Header	Data three	Data four
Third Row header	Data five	Data six

Turn off all the default style options in the Table Style Options group by clicking Header Row, First Column, and Banded Rows to remove the bolding and distinctive borders:

First Column Header	Second Column Header	Third Column header
First Row Header	Data one	Data two
Second Row Header	Data three	Data four
Third Row header	Data five	Data six

In the Table Styles group, select the fifth style from the left (second from the right), and even shading is applied to the entire table. Click Header Row and then First Column to have a darker color applied to each of those areas. Finally, click Banded Rows to accent rows, as shown next.

First Column Header	Second Column Header	Third Column header
First Row Header	Data one	Data two
Second Row Header	Data three	Data four
Third Row header	Data five	Data six

Click Change Colors and select a different color set for the table.

Apply Shading

The color shading is independent of any styles. Use it to shade any set of cells. Select a cell, a row, a column, or the entire table, click Cell Shading in the Table Tools Design tab, and click the color you want to use.

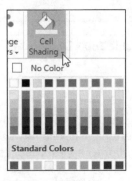

 You can copy and paste an entire table or a single cell (assuming you have first inserted a new column or row in which to paste the cell) as you would copy and paste any other object in Word, but copying and pasting both rows and columns requires that you have set aside the required space in the table where the copy is going.

6

Entering, Editing, and Formatting Data in Excel Online

HOW TO...

- Explore Excel data types
- Enter and format data
- Add and remove data
- Select, edit, and delete data
- Select cells and ranges
- Copy and paste data
- Work with rows and column
- Format cells with color and borders
- Align text

Data is the heart and soul of Excel, yet before you can calculate data, chart it review it, and otherwise *use* it, you have to place it on a worksheet. Data comes in several forms—such as numbers, text, dates, and times—and Excel handles the entry of each form uniquely. After you enter data into Excel's worksheets, you might want to make changes. Simple actions—such as removing text and numbers, copying and pasting, and moving data—are much more enhanced in Excel than in other programs that you might be familiar with.

In this chapter, you will learn how to add and delete cells, rows, and columns, and how to change their appearance.

Enter and Format Numbers, Text, Dates, and Times

An Excel worksheet is a matrix, or grid, of rows (that run horizontally, or across the sheet) and columns (that run vertically, or up and down). Across the top of every worksheet are lettered *column headings*; numbered *row headings* are displayed along the left side of the worksheet. The first row of a typical worksheet is used for column *headers*, information that you type in. These headers represent categories of similar data. The rows beneath a column header contain data that may be further categorized by a row header along the leftmost column or simply listed below the column header. Worksheets can also be used to set up *tables* of data, where columns are sometimes referred to as *fields* and each row represents a unique *record* of data. Figure 6-1 shows examples of two common worksheet arrangements.

Each intersection of a row and column is called a *cell* and is referenced first by the column location and then by the row location. The combination of a column letter and row number assigns each cell an *address*. For example, the cell at the intersection of column D and row 8 is called D8. A cell is considered *active* when it is clicked or otherwise selected as the place in which to place new data.

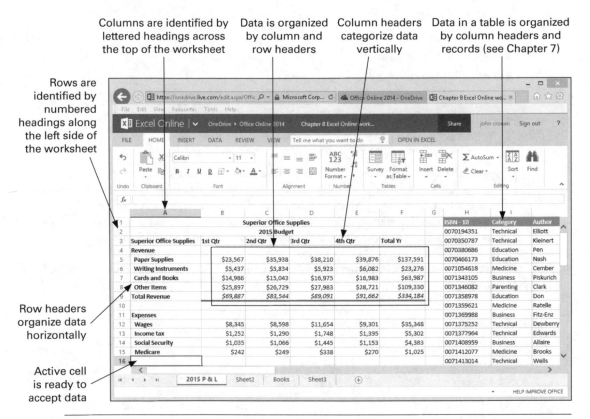

FIGURE 6-1 The grid layout of Excel worksheets is defined by several components.

Explore Excel Data Types

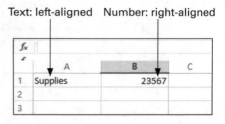

Cells in Excel are characterized by the type of data they contain. *Text* is composed of characters that cannot be used in calculations. For example, "Quarterly revenue is not meeting projection" is text, and so is "1302 Grand Ave." *Numbers* are just that: numerical characters that can be used in calculations. *Dates* and *times* occupy a special category of numbers that can be used in calculations and are handled in a variety of ways. Excel lets you know what it thinks a cell contains by its default alignment of a cell's contents—that is, text is left-aligned and numbers (including dates and times) are right-aligned by default (of course, you can change these, as described later in the chapter in the section "Align Cell Contents").

Enter Text

In an Excel worksheet, text is used to identify, explain, and emphasize numeric data. It comprises characters that cannot be used in calculations. You enter text by clicking a cell and typing, just as you would in a word-processing program. When you click in a cell, it becomes the *active* cell. Excel provides several highly visible identifiers for the active cell: the column and row headings are highlighted, the Formula bar displays the cell contents, and the cell borders are bold.

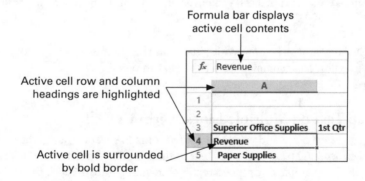

Enter Text Continuously

Text (and numbers) that are too long to fit in one cell width will appear to spread into the adjoining cells to the right of the active cell. These cells have not been "used," however; their contents have just been hidden under the active text, as shown in Figure 6-2.

To enter text on one line, follow these steps:

1. Click in the cell where you want the text to start.
2. Type the text. The text displays in one or more cells (see rows 2 and 4 in Figure 6-2).
3. Complete the entry. (See "Complete an Entry" later in the chapter for several ways to do that.)

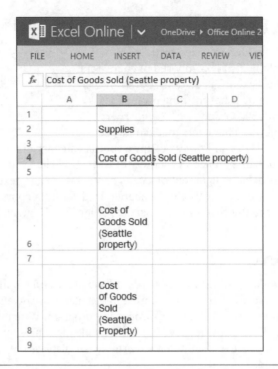

FIGURE 6-2   Text in a cell can cover several cells or be placed on multiple lines.

Note See "Adjust Column Width" later in this chapter for ways to increase the column width to accommodate all the text in a cell.

Wrap Text on Multiple Lines Within a Cell

You can select a cell and wrap text so that it fits in several lines in the same cell, much as a word-processing program wraps text to the next line when entered text reaches the right margin. An example of wrapped text is shown in Figure 6-2, cell B6.

1. Click the cell where you want to enter text.
2. Type all the text you want to appear in a cell. The text will continue to the right, overlapping as many cells as its length dictates (see row 4 in Figure 6-2).
3. Press ENTER to complete the entry. (See "Complete an Entry" later in the chapter.) Click the cell to select it.
4. Click the Home tab at the left side of the ribbon. In the Alignment group, click the Wrap Text button. The text wraps within the confines of the column width, increasing the row height as necessary (see cell B6 in Figure 6-2).

Constrain Text on Multiple Lines

When you want to constrain the length of text in a cell, follow these steps:

1. Click the cell where you want to enter text.
2. Type the text you want to appear on the first line.
3. Press ALT-ENTER. The text disappears from the cell temporarily and is ready to accept a new line of text.
4. Repeat steps 2 and 3 for any additional lines of text. (See row 8 in Figure 6-2.)
5. Complete the entry. (See "Complete an Entry.")

Complete an Entry

You can complete an entry using touch, the mouse, or the keyboard and control which cell will be the next active cell.

- **Move the active cell to the right**   To complete the entry and move to the next cell in the same row, press TAB.
- **Move the active cell to the next row**   To complete the entry and move the active cell to the next row, press ENTER. The active cell moves to the *beginning cell* in the next row (see the note that follows this list).

$1,035	$1,066	$1,445
$242	$249	$338

- **Move the active cell to any cell**   To complete the entry and move the active cell to any cell in the worksheet, click or tap the cell you want to become active.

 The *beginning cell* is located in the same column where you first started entering data. So, for example, if you started entering data in cell A5 and continued through E5, pressing TAB between entries A5 through D5 and pressing ENTER in E5, the active cell would move to A6 (the first cell in the next row). If, however, you started entering data in cell C5, pressing TAB between entries C5 through G5, after pressing ENTER at the end of that row of entries, the active cell would move to C6, the cell below where you started.

Enter Numeric Data

Numbers, from the simplest to the most complex, are numeric data. Excel provides several features to help you work more easily with numbers used to represent values in various categories, such as currency, accounting, and mathematics.

Enter Numbers

Enter numbers by selecting a cell and typing the numbers.

1. Click the cell where you want the numbers entered.
2. Type the numbers. Use decimal places, thousands separators, and other formatting as you type, or have Excel format these things for you. (See "Format Numbers" later in this chapter.)
3. Complete the entry. (See "Complete an Entry.")

You can cause a number to be interpreted by Excel as text and be left-aligned by formatting the number as text. Address numbers, Social Security numbers, and other numbers that don't require calculation are examples of these types of numbers. (See "Format Numbers" later in this chapter.)

ISBN - 10	Category
0070194351	Technical
0070350787	Technical
0070380686	Education

Enter Numbers Using Scientific Notation

Exponents are used in scientific notation to shorten (or round off) very large or small numbers. The shorthand scientific notation display does not affect how the number is used in calculations; however, rounding provides a less precise result when moving a decimal point several orders of magnitude. (To retain precision, see the associated tip regarding converting numbers to scientific notation.)

To enter numbers using scientific notation, follow these steps:

1. Click the cell where you want the data entered.
2. Type the number using three components:
   - **Base** For example, 4, 7.56, −2.5
   - **Scientific notation identifier** Type the letter "e."
   - **Exponent** The number of times 10 is multiplied by itself. Positive exponent numbers increment the base number to the right of the decimal point, negative numbers to the left. For example, scientific notation for the number 123,456,789.0 is written to two decimal places as 1.23×10^8. In Excel, you would type **1.23e8**.
3. After you complete the entry (see "Complete an Entry"), it will display as shown:

You can convert a number to scientific notation from the Home tab Number group on the ribbon. Click the Number Format down arrow, and click Scientific near the bottom of the list. To set the number of decimal places, click the Increase Decimal or Decrease Decimal button in the Number group.

Enter and Format Dates

If you can think of a way to enter a date, Excel can probably recognize it as such. For example, Table 6-1 shows how Excel handles different ways to make the date entry. For example, use the date of March 1, 2015 (assuming it is sometime in 2015), in a worksheet. If the year is omitted, Excel assumes the current year.

 When changing from a Short Date format to a Long Date format, you may see a cell full of pound symbols instead of the expected date. To display the Long Date format correctly, increase the column width to accommodate the longer date. (See "Adjust Column Width" later in the chapter.)

| 2/2/2015 | Monday, February 2, 2015 | ########## |

You can change how a date is displayed in Excel by choosing a new format:

1. Select the cell that contains the date you want to change. (See "Select Cells and Ranges" later in the chapter to see how to apply formats to more than one cell at a time.)
2. Select Number Format in the Home tab Number group. From the drop-down list, as shown in Figure 6-3, select Short Date or Long Date. The date will display in the selected format.

 You can change how dates and times appear in Office Online documents by changing your language settings (for example, to change from day/month/year to month/day/year). On the onedrive.com web page, select your user name in the upper-right corner of the screen and select Account Settings. Sign in (if necessary) and select the current language setting in the status bar—for example, English (United States). Open the drop-down list of language preferences, select the one whose format you want, and click Save.

English (United States)   © 2014 Microsoft

TABLE 6-1 Examples of Excel Date Formats

Typing This	Displays This After Completing the Entry
3/1, 3-1, 1-mar, or 1-Mar	1-Mar
3/1/15, 3-1-15, 3/1/2015, 3-1-2015, 3-1/15, or 3-1/2015	3/1/2015
Mar 1, 15; March 1, 2015; 1-mar-15; or 1-Mar-2015	1-Mar-15

FIGURE 6-3 You can choose the Short Date or Long Date format to display dates in Excel.

Format Numbers

You can format numbers in a cell in any one of several numeric categories, as described in Table 6-2 (Date, Time, Scientific, and Text formats are described elsewhere in this chapter).

 Although the appearance of a number will change using different formats, the value of the number that appears in the Formula bar when the cell is selected remains the same in calculations.

To format numbers in a cell, follow these steps:

1. Select the cells to which you want to apply the new format.
2. Select Number Format from the Home tab Number group.
3. Select the number format you want from the drop-down list (see Figure 6-3).
4. Apply additional formatting attributes by adding or decreasing decimal places, or adding a comma to separate thousands, by selecting the appropriate button in the Number group.

 Formatting also can be applied to cells in advance of entering numbers (or text) so that the attributes are displayed as you complete the entry. To do this, select the cells and apply the formatting. See "Select Cells and Ranges" later in the chapter for ways to select cells.

TABLE 6-2   Predefined Number Formats

Number Format	Description
General	The default number format, rounds off numbers if they don't fit in a cell's width, and converts to scientific notation numbers with 12 or more digits (see "Enter Numbers Using Scientific Notation" earlier in the chapter).
Number	Similar to the General format, but differs in how decimals are shown in some numbers. For example, the Number formatted 643.00 displays as 643 formatted as General, and longer decimals are rounded off to two places using Number formatting. For example, 12.1234 (General) displays as 12.12 (Number).
Currency	Adds a currency symbol (such as $) to the number and activates the Increase Decimal and Decrease Decimal buttons to change the number of decimal places.
Accounting	Similar to the Currency format, but also aligns in a column the currency symbol and decimal point.
Percentage	Adds the percentage symbol (%) after multiplying the number by 100 and activates the Increase Decimal and Decrease Decimal buttons to change the number of decimal places.
Fraction	Changes a decimal number to a fraction. For example, 0.5 converts to 1/2.

Work with Dates and Times

Dates and times in Excel are assigned values so that they can be used in calculations. (Chapter 7 describes how to use formulas and functions.) Dates are assigned a serial value starting with January 1, 1900 (serial value 1). The number you see on the Formula bar is the value of the date in the active cell (you can convert a date to its serial value by changing the format from Long Date/Short Date to Number). For example, January 1, 2015, has a serial value of 42,005. Times are converted to the decimal equivalent of a day. For example, 4:15 P.M. is converted to 0.68.

Because Excel considers dates and times as numeric values, they are right-aligned in a cell. If you see what you think is a date but it is left-aligned, Excel is treating it as text, not a date, and you would receive an error message if you tried to use it in a formula (see Chapter 7).

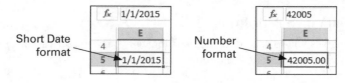

Use Times

Excel's conventions for time are as follows:

- Colons (:) are used as separators between hours, minutes, and seconds.
- A.M. is assumed unless you specify P.M. or when you enter a time from 12:00 to 12:59.
- A.M. and P.M. do not display in the cell if they are not entered.
- You specify P.M. by entering a space followed by "p," "P," "pm," or "PM."
- Seconds are not displayed in the cell if not entered.
- A.M., P.M., and seconds are displayed in the Formula bar of a cell that contains a time.

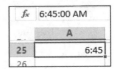

Enter Times

Enter time values with these steps:

1. Select the cell in which you want to enter a time.
2. Type the hour followed by a colon.
3. Type the minutes followed by a colon.
4. Type the seconds, if needed.
5. Type a space and **PM**, if needed.
6. Complete the entry.

Format Times

You can change a number to the time format from the Number Format drop-down list. (See "Work with Dates and Times" for information on how Excel converts numbers to time.)

1. Select the cell that contains the number you want to change. (See "Select Cells and Ranges" later in the chapter for how to apply formats to more than one cell at a time.)
2. Select Number Format in the Home tab Number group.
3. From the Number Format drop-down list, select the Time format.

Add Data Quickly

Excel provides several features that help you quickly add more data to existing data with a minimum of keystrokes. For example, Excel will complete an entry for you after you type the first few characters of data that appear in a previous entry in the same column. Simply press ENTER to accept the completed entry.

Fill Data into Adjoining Cells

Excel enables you to copy data that isn't logically part of a series (for example, names of months and days of the week) into adjoining cells.

1. Select the cell that contains the data you want to copy into adjoining cells.
2. Point to the fill handle in the lower-right corner of the cell. The pointer turns into a cross.

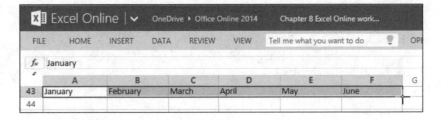

FIGURE 6-4   You can quickly continue a series (January through June, in this case) to create headings by dragging the fill handle.

3. Drag the handle in the direction you want to extend the data until you've reached the last cell in the range you want to fill.

Continue a Series of Data

Data can be *logically* extended into one or more adjoining cells. For example, 1 and 2 extend to 3, 4, 5, and so on; Tuesday extends to Wednesday, Thursday, Friday, and so on; January extends to February, March, April, and so on; and 2014 and 2015 extend to 2016, 2017, 2018, and so on. Here's how to continue a series of data:

1. Select the cell or cells that contain a partial series. (See "Select Cells and Ranges" later in the chapter for more information on selecting more than one cell.)
2. Point to the fill handle in the lower-right corner of the last cell. The pointer turns into a cross.
3. Drag the handle in the direction you want until you've reached the last cell in the range to complete the series; then release to fill the cells, as shown in Figure 6-4.

Select, Edit, Copy, Paste, and Delete Data

The data-intensive nature of Excel necessitates easy ways to change, copy, or remove data already entered on a worksheet. In addition, Excel has facilities to help you find and replace data.

Edit Cell Data

You have several choices on how to edit data, depending on whether you want to replace all the contents of a cell or just part of the contents, and whether you want to do it in the cell or in the Formula bar.

Edit Cell Contents

You can edit data entered in a cell in two ways. Here is the first way:

1. Double-click the text in the cell where you want to begin editing. An insertion point is placed in the cell.

2. Move the insertion point where you want new text to appear and type the new data. Select the characters you want to overwrite or delete using touch or a pointing device, or use keyboard shortcuts.
3. Complete the entry when you've finished. (See "Complete an Entry" earlier in the chapter.)

And here is the second way:

1. Select the cell to edit.
2. Select the cell's contents in the Formula bar where you want to make changes.
3. Type the new data. Select characters to overwrite or delete using touch or a pointing device, or use keyboard shortcuts.
4. Press ENTER or tap outside of the Formula bar to complete the entry.

Replace All Cell Contents

To replace all the contents within a cell, simply select the cell and type the new data. The original data is deleted and replaced by your new characters.

Cancel Cell Editing

 Before you complete a cell entry, you can revert back to your original data by pressing ESC or selecting Undo from the Home tab Undo group.

Remove Cell Contents

You can easily delete cell contents, move them to other cells, or clear selective attributes of a cell.

 To undo a data-removal action, even if you have performed several actions since removing the data, click Undo in the Home tab Undo group (or press CTRL-Z) for the most recent action. For earlier actions, continue clicking Undo to work your way back.

Remove Data

A cell can contain several components, including the following:

- **Formats** Consisting of number formats and borders
- **Contents** Consisting of formulas and data
- **Comments** Consisting of notes you attach to a cell
- **Hyperlinks** Consisting of links to other ranges on the current worksheet, other worksheets in the current workbook, other workbooks or other files, and web pages in web sites

You can selectively remove all contents from a cell including formatting, remove formatting only, or remove only the cell contents (retaining cell formatting). You can apply these actions to more than one cell by selecting the cells or the cell range. (See "Select Cells and Ranges" for more information on selecting various configurations.)

- To remove the contents of cells, select Clear in the Home tab Editing group; then select Clear Contents, or press DELETE.
- To remove only formatting from cells, select Clear in the Home tab Editing group, and then select Clear Formats.
- To remove contents and formatting from cells, select Clear in the Home tab Editing group, and then select Clear All.

 If you use the Delete button in the Home tab Cells group, you delete the selected cells' contents *and* the cells themselves from the worksheet. See Chapter 7 for more information on deleting cells.

Move Data

Cell contents can be removed from one location and placed in another location of equal size. First select the cell or range you want to move. Then do one of the following:

- Place the pointer on any edge of the selection, except the lower-right corner where the Fill handle resides, until it turns into a cross with arrowhead tips. Drag the cell or range to the new location, as shown in Figure 6-5.
- On the Home tab Clipboard group, click Cut. Select the new location, and click the Paste button in the Clipboard group. (See "Copy and Paste Data" later in this chapter for more information on pasting options.)

11	Expenses		
12	Wages	$8,345	$8,598
13	Income tax	$1,252	$1,290
14	Social Security	$1,035	$1,066
15	Medicare	$242	$249
16			
17			
18			
19			
20			
21			

FIGURE 6-5 Move selected cells by dragging an edge of the selection border.

Select Cells and Ranges

The key to many actions in Excel is the ability to select cells in various configurations and use them to perform calculations and operations. You can select a single cell and adjacent cells (or *ranges*).

- **Select a single cell**   Select a cell by clicking it. Or move to a cell using the arrow keys or by completing an entry in a cell above or to the left.
- **Select a range of adjacent cells**   Select a cell and drag over the additional cells you want to include in the range. Or select the first cell in the range, press and hold SHIFT, and click the last cell in the range. Or select the first cell in the range, press and hold SHIFT, and press the arrow keys to move the selection in the direction you need to select the range you want.
- **Select a row or column**   Click a row (number) heading or column (letter) heading. Or select a cell and press SHIFT-SPACE to select its row; press CTRL-SPACE to select its column.
- **Select adjacent rows or columns**   Drag down the row headings or across the column headings.
- **Resize an adjacent selection**   Press SHIFT and click the cell you want to be at the end of the selection.

   To select larger numbers of adjacent cells, rows, or columns, click the first item in the group, and then press SHIFT while clicking the last item in the group.

Copy and Paste Data

You can copy data you've already entered on a worksheet (or in other programs) to the same or other worksheets, or even to other Windows applications. You first *copy* the data to the Windows Clipboard, where it is temporarily stored. After selecting a destination for the data, you *paste* it into the cell or cells. You can copy all or part of the data in a cell. You can paste it on your worksheet one time, in one location, or at different locations several times. (The copied data remains on the Clipboard until you replace it with another copy action. See the related tip for cut actions.) Although many computer users are familiar with a basic copy, Excel's paste feature lets you selectively paste attributes of the data. Also, data copied and pasted within a workbook will retain its formatting such as bolding, while data copied from outside sources and pasted into Excel appears as plain text—that is, without its original formatting.

   Another way to send information to the Clipboard is to *cut* the data. When you cut data, like a copy action, information is placed on the Clipboard and removes any existing data already there. However, when you cut data, it is removed from its original location (it's essentially moved), unlike copying, where the data is retained at its original location.

Copy Data

Copy data with these steps:

1. Select the cells that contain the data you want to copy; or double-click a cell and select the characters you want to copy.

2. In the Home tab Clipboard group, click Copy. Or, from the keyboard, press CTRL-C. In either case, the selected data is copied to the Clipboard, and the border around the cells displays a moving dotted line.

 When you first start using the Clipboard from Office Online apps, you may see a message asking if you want to allow the web page to access your Clipboard. If you want to allow this, click Allow Access; otherwise, click Don't Allow.

Paste Data

Once data is placed on the Clipboard through a *copy* action, you can selectively include or omit formulas, values, and formatting *before* you paste or move data. (See Chapter 9 for information on formulas, values, and arithmetic operations.)

 Even after you paste the data, if you change your mind, just click the Undo button.

To paste data, do the following:

1. Select the location (a cell or range) in which to place the cut or copied data.
2. On the Home tab Clipboard group, click Paste (the upper half of the Paste button), or press CTRL-V, to insert all aspects of the copied data. To insert selective aspects of the copied data, click the Paste down arrow (the lower half of the Paste button) and select from the pasting options that appear.

Alternatively, you can right-click the selected cell or range, and on the context menu, click Paste to insert all aspects of the copied data.

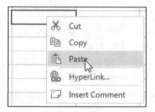

3. After the paste, the data is inserted in the new cell or range, as shown in Figure 6-6.
4. Repeat steps 1 and 2 to paste the copied data to other locations. Press ESC when you're finished to remove the flashing border around the source cells.

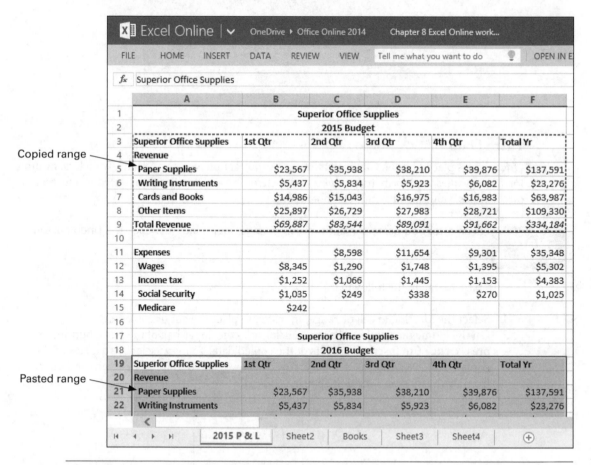

FIGURE 6-6 Pasting cells and ranges allow you to move data around a worksheet, within a workbook, or to other documents.

If you paste data into a cell that contains existing data, that existing data will be replaced with the pasted data. To avoid losing data, insert blank cells, rows, and columns to accommodate the data you are pasting. See "Add and Remove Rows, Columns, and Cells" later in this chapter for more information on inserting cells, rows, and columns.

Find Data

In worksheets that might span thousands of rows and columns (more than 1 million rows and 16,000 columns are possible), you need the ability to locate data quickly.

Here's how to find data:

1. In the Home tab Editing group, click Find to open the Find dialog box, as shown in Figure 6-7.
2. Type the text or number you want to find in the Find What text box.
3. Choose whether to search the worksheet Up (above) or Down (below) the active cells.
4. Click Find, and Excel will display the area of the worksheet where the first instance of the search data is found. Click Find again to find multiple instances of the data. Alternatively, you can press CTRL-F (twice if the first time it opens the Find dialog box) to display a Find toolbar above Excel's title bar, as shown in Figure 6-8. Here, as you begin tying in your search criteria, Excel highlights the data in the worksheet that contains your entry. You can filter the search to have Excel find only whole word/ number instances and only the same case (uppercase/lowercase) when searching for data that contains letters.

 The Go To dialog box (CTRL-G) enables you to find cells and ranges by name or address. Using the Go To dialog box is covered in Chapter 9.

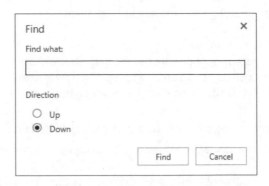

FIGURE 6-7 You can quickly scan a worksheet to locate data above or below the currently selected cells.

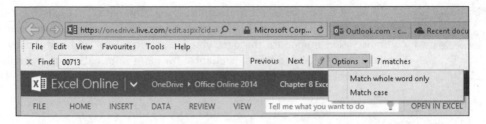

FIGURE 6-8   The Find toolbar provides real-time search and offers more features than the Find dialog box.

Select, Size, Add, Hide, and Remove Rows and Columns

Getting a worksheet to look the way you want will probably involve adding and removing cells, rows, and/or columns to separate your data and remove unwanted space appropriately. You might also want to adjust the size and type of cell borders and add comments to provide ancillary information about the contents of a cell. This section covers these features and more.

   Don't ever worry about running out of rows or columns in a worksheet. You can have up to 1,048,576 rows and 16,384 columns in each Excel worksheet. As a bit of tourist information, the last cell address in a worksheet is XFD1048576.

Adjust Row Height

You can change the height of a row manually or by changing cell contents.

Change Row Height by Dragging

Use these steps to change the row height by dragging:

1. Select one or more rows.
2. Point (using a mouse pointer) at or tap the bottom border of a selected row heading until the pointer changes to a cross with up and down arrowheads.
3. Drag the border up or down to the row height you want.

Change Row Height by Changing Cell Contents

Use these steps to change the row height by changing cell contents:

1. Select one or more cells, rows, or characters that you want to change in height.
2. Change the cell contents. Following are examples of the various ways to do this:
   - **Changing font size**   In the Home tab Font group, click the Font Size down arrow, and click a size from the drop-down list. If you have already manually changed the row height, however, changing the font size of a cell's contents will not automatically change the row height.

- **Placing characters on two or more lines within a cell**   Place the insertion point at the end of a line or where you want the line to break, and press ALT-ENTER.

When a selected object changes size or a new object is inserted, if its height becomes larger than the original row height, the height of all cells in the row(s) will be increased. The size of the other cell's contents, however, stays the same.

Return Row Height to Fit the Size of Cell Contents

Excel automatically adjusts row height to accommodate the largest object or text size added to a row. If you subsequently remove larger objects or text, you need to resize to fit the remaining objects. See "Change Row Height by Dragging."

Adjust Column Width

As with changing row height, you can change the width of a column manually or by changing cell contents. The default column width for a worksheet is determined by the average number of characters in the default font that will fit in the column (not in points, as with row height). For example, the default Calibri 11 pt. font provides a standard column width of 8.43 characters.

Change the Width by Dragging

Use these steps to change the column width by dragging:

1. Select one or more columns.
2. Point (using a mouse pointer) at or tap the right border of a selected column heading until the pointer changes to a cross with left and right arrowheads.

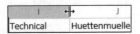

3. Drag the border to the left or right to the width you want.

 You cannot change the width of a single cell without changing the width of all cells in the column.

Change Column Width to Fit the Size of Cell Contents

Double-click the right border of the column header for the column or selected columns. The column width(s) will adjust to fit the longest entry.

Hide and Unhide Rows and Columns

Hiding rows and columns provides a means to remove rows or columns from view temporarily, without deleting them or their contents.

Hide Rows and Columns

Use these steps to hide rows and columns:

1. Select the rows or columns to be hidden.
2. Right-click the selected items, and click Hide Rows or Hide Columns.
   Alternatively, drag the bottom border of the row header of the rows to be hidden *up*, or drag the right border of the column header of the columns to be hidden to the *left*. The row numbers or column letters of the hidden cells are omitted, as shown in Figure 6-9. (You can tell cells are hidden by the small space in the row or column headers between the hidden rows or columns.)

Unhide Rows or Columns

Use these steps to unhide rows or columns:

1. Drag across the row or column headings on both sides of the hidden rows or columns to select them. For example, in Figure 6-9, you would drag across rows 5 and 9, and columns H and K.
2. Right-click the selection and click Unhide Rows or Unhide Columns.

If you hide one or more rows or columns beginning with column A or row 1, you won't be able to drag across the rows or columns on both sides of the hidden rows or columns to unhide them. However, you can select the hidden row or column by selecting the row or column below or to the right, respectively, of the hidden row or column and dragging the selection into the row or column heading. Then, when you right-click and select Unhide Rows or Unhide Columns from the context menu, the hidden row or column will appear.

A small space between rows and columns identifies hidden rows and columns

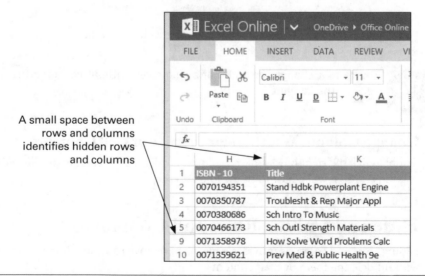

FIGURE 6-9   Rows 6, 7, and 8 and columns I and J are hidden in this worksheet.

Add and Remove Rows, Columns, and Cells

You can insert or delete rows, columns, or cells one at a time or select adjacent items to perform these actions on groups of them. Select rows and columns by clicking their respective numbered and lettered headers.

Add a Single Row

Use these steps to add a single row:

1. Select the row below where you want the new row placed.
2. In the Home tab Cells group, click the Insert icon (the upper part of the Insert tool), or right-click the cell header in the selected row and click Insert Rows.

Add Multiple Adjacent Rows

Use these steps to add multiple adjacent rows:

1. Select the number of rows you want in the row of cells immediately below the row where you want the new rows to appear. For example, if you want to add four rows below row 6, select rows 7–10.
2. In the Home tab Cells group, click the Insert down arrow and click Insert Rows; or right-click a cell in the selected rows and click Insert Rows.

Add a Single Column

Use these steps to add a single column:

1. Select the column to the right of where you want the new column to appear.
2. In the Home tab Cells group, click the Insert icon (the upper part of the Insert tool), or right-click the column header in the selected column and click Insert Columns.

Add Multiple Adjacent Columns

Use these steps to add multiple adjacent columns:

1. Select the number of columns you want immediately to the right of the column where you want the new columns to appear.
2. In the Home tab Cells group, click the Insert down arrow and click Insert Columns; or right-click a cell in the selected columns and click Insert Columns.

Add Cells

Use these steps to add cells:

1. Select the cells adjacent to where you want to insert the new cells.
2. In the Home tab Cells group, click the Insert down arrow. Then do one of the following:
   - Click Insert Cells & Shift Right to move existing cells to the right.
   - Click Insert Cells & Shift Down to move existing cells down.

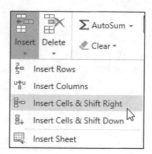

Remove Cells, Rows, and Columns

Use these steps to remove cells, rows, and columns:

1. Select the single or adjacent items (cells, rows, or columns) you want to remove.
2. In the Home tab Cells group, click the Delete icon. Selected rows are removed and remaining rows move up to fill their place; selected columns are removed and remaining columns move left; and selected cells have their contents removed.
3. To remove cells and fill their place with existing cells, click the Insert down arrow and then do one of the following:
   - Click Delete Cells & Shift Left to move existing cells to the left.
   - Click Delete Cells & Shift Up to move existing cells up.

Merge Cells

Use these steps to merge cells:

1. Select the cells you want to combine into one cell; for example, you can create one long cell across your column headers and center a title in it as shown here.

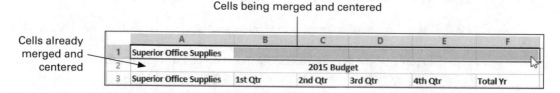

2. In the Home tab Alignment group, click Merge & Center.

Format Using Borders, Alignment, and Color

You can do a lot to make your worksheets look attractive by adding color, borders, and alignment.

Add Color

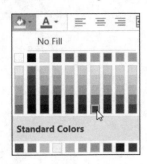

You can enhance your worksheets by adding color to cells to highlight headers and other important data. Select the cells you want to fill with a color, and in the Home tab Font group, click Fill Color and then click a color from one of the palettes.

Change Cell Borders

Borders provide a quick and effective way to emphasize and segregate data on a worksheet.

1. Select the cell, range, row, or column whose border you want modify.
2. In the Home tab Font group, click the Borders button and select the border style you want. (The style you choose remains as the available border style on the button.)
3. To remove a border, select the cell(s), click the Borders button, and click No Border.

Align Cell Contents

You can align the contents (both text and numbers) of cells and merged cells (see "Merge Cells" earlier in the chapter), both horizontally and vertically.

1. Select the cells whose text you want to align.
2. In the Home tab Alignment group, select from one of the three vertical cell alignments: Top Align, Middle Align, or Bottom Align. Select from one of the three horizontal cell alignments: Align Text Left, Center, or Align Text Right.

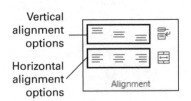

Vertical alignment options

Horizontal alignment options

Alignment

7

Using Formulas, Functions, and Tables and Organizing Data

HOW TO...

- Reference cells
- Work with formulas
- Use functions
- Work with tables
- Organize data with worksheets

Excel enables you to perform powerful calculations easily using formulas and functions. *Formulas* are mathematical statements that follow a set of rules and use a specific syntax. In this chapter you will learn how to reference and locate cells used in formulas, and how to build and work with formulas. *Functions*—readymade formulas that you can use to get quick results for specific applications, such as figuring out loan payments—are also covered. Tables, though available in Word and PowerPoint, take on a greater role with expanded capabilities in Excel, as you will see. Finally, techniques are presented to help you better organize your data using sorting and filtering and by adding worksheets.

Reference and Name Cells and Ranges of Cells

Formulas typically make use of data already entered in worksheets and need a scheme to locate, or *reference*, that data. You can use shortcuts to help you recall addresses as well as a *syntax*, or set of rules, to communicate to Excel how you want cells used.

Work with Cell Referencing Types

Formulas use three basic methods and one extended method for referencing cells; these adhere to the Excel default "A1" cell reference scheme used in this book.

- **Relative references**   Move with cells as they are copied or moved around a worksheet. This is the most flexible and common way to use cell references and is the Excel default, such that the cell in the first row and first column of a sheet is referenced as A1 in the Formula bar. Therefore, if you sum a list of revenue items for the first quarter (see Figure 7-1), you would see "=SUM(B5:B8)" in the Formula bar. If you then copy and paste that summary cell to the summary cells for the other three quarters, Excel will deduce that you want the totals for the other quarters to be =SUM(C5:C8), =SUM(D5:D8), and =SUM(E5:E8). Figure 7-1 shows how this appears on the worksheet for C9, D9, E9, and F9.
- **Absolute references**   Do not change cell addresses when you copy or move formulas. Absolute references are displayed in the Formula bar with the dollar sign preceding the reference—for example, A1. In Figure 7-1, C9 was copied from B9 using absolute referencing.

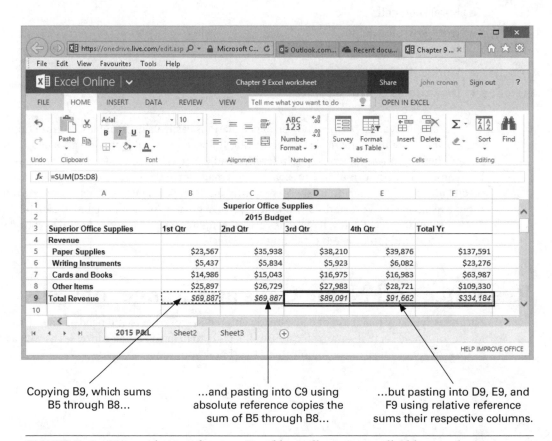

Copying B9, which sums B5 through B8...

...and pasting into C9 using absolute reference copies the sum of B5 through B8...

...but pasting into D9, E9, and F9 using relative reference sums their respective columns.

FIGURE 7-1   Using relative references, Excel logically assumes cell addresses change in copied formulas, whereas absolute references do not change from their original address.

- **Mixed references**   Include one relative and one absolute cell reference. Such references are displayed in the worksheet and Formula bar with a dollar sign preceding the absolute reference but no dollar sign before the relative reference. For example, $A1 indicates absolute column, relative row; A$1 indicates relative column, absolute row.
- **External (or 3-D) references**   An extended form of relative, absolute, and mixed cell references. They are used when referencing cells from other worksheets or workbooks. Such a reference might look like this in the Formula bar: [*workbook name*]*worksheet name*!A1.

Note   In the desktop version of Excel, you can view formulas instead of cell values, but Excel Online doesn't support this feature. If you try to open a workbook that was saved with formulas displayed instead of values, you will receive an error message and won't be able to open the workbook.

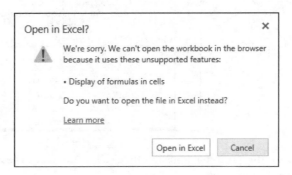

Change Cell References

To change cell referencing, follow these steps:

1. Select the cell that contains the formula reference you want to change.
2. Edit the cell address by entering or removing the dollar symbol ($) in front of row and/or column identifiers. Your choices for cell references are
   - Absolute (A1)
   - Mixed (relative column, absolute row) (A$1)
   - Mixed (absolute column, relative row) ($A1)
   - Relative (A1)

Tip   Absolute cell references are typically used when you want to copy the values of cells and are not interested in applying their formulas to other cells, such as in a summary or report where the relative references would be meaningless. Although you can apply absolute reference syntax to each cell reference, a faster way is to select a destination cell, click the Paste down arrow in the Home tab Clipboard group, and then click Paste Values. See "Copy Formulas" later in the chapter for more information on copying and pasting formulas.

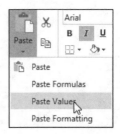

Use Cell Reference Operators

Cell reference operators (colons, commas, and spaces used in an address, such as E5:E10 E16:E17,E12) provide the syntax for referencing cell ranges, unions, and intersections.

Reference a Range   A *range* defines a block of contiguous cells. Type a colon (:) between the upper-leftmost cell and the lower-rightmost cell (for example, B5:C8).

Define a range in a formula by typing
a colon between the upper-leftmost
and lower-rightmost cells.

	B	C	
fx	=SUM(B5:C8)		
1		Superior Office Supplies	
2		2015 Budget	
3	1st Qtr	2nd Qtr	3rd Qtr
4			
5	$23,567	$35,938	
6	$5,437	$5,834	
7	$14,986	$15,043	
8	$25,897	$26,729	
9	$69,887	$83,544	

Reference a Union   A *union* joins multiple cell references. Type a comma (,) between separate cell references (for example, B5,B7,C6).

	B	C	
fx	=SUM(B5,C6,B7)		
1		Superior Office Supplies	
2		2015 Budget	
3	1st Qtr	2nd Qtr	3rd Qtr
4			
5	$23,567	$35,938	
6	$5,437	$5,834	
7	$14,986	$15,043	
8	$25,897	$26,729	
9	$69,887	$83,544	

Reference an Intersection   An *intersection* is the overlapping, or common, cells in two ranges. Type a space (press the SPACEBAR) between two range-cell references (for example, B5:B8 B7:C8, where B7 and B8 are the common cells).

f_x	=SUM(B5:B8 B7:C8)	
	B	C
1		Superior Office Supplies
2		2015 Budget
3	1st Qtr	2nd Qtr	3rd Qtr
4		
5	$23,567	$35,938
6	$5,437	$5,834
7	$14,986	$15,043
8	$25,897	$26,729
9	$69,887	$83,544

Go to a Cell Quickly

When you're building formulas, it's very handy to be able to locate cells quickly that you want to reference. You can locate any cell using its cell address. Additionally, in the desktop version of Excel you can name a cell (MonthTotal, for example) or a range to refer to physical cell addresses, and then use the names when referencing the cell in formulas and functions. (Names are more descriptive, easier to remember, and often quicker to enter than A1-style cell references.) Although you cannot name a cell in Excel Online, you can quickly locate named cells in workbooks that were created in desktop Excel:

1. Press CTRL-G to open the Go To dialog box.
2. In the Reference text box, type the cell or range address or the name of the cell on the current or another worksheet in the same workbook that you want to locate. Then click OK.

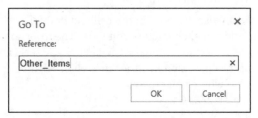

The worksheet moves (if necessary) to display the area around the referenced cell and the referenced cell or range is selected.

Build, Edit, Copy, Move, and Calculate Formulas

Formulas are mathematical equations that combine *values* and *cell references* with *operators* to calculate a result. Values are actual numbers or logical values, such as True and False, or the contents of cells that contain numbers or logical values. Cell references point to cells whose values are to be used, for example, E5:E10, E12, and MonthlyTot. Operators, such as + (add), > (greater than), and ^ (use an exponent), tell Excel what type of calculation to perform or logical comparison to apply. Prebuilt formulas, or *functions*, that return a value also can be used in formulas. (Functions are described later in this chapter in the section "Use Functions.")

Create a Formula

You create formulas by either entering or referencing values. The character that tells Excel to perform a calculation is the equal sign (=), and it must precede any combination of values, cell references, and operators.

Excel formulas are calculated from left to right according to an ordered hierarchy of operators. For example, exponents (10^4, or 10^4) precede multiplication and division, which precede addition and subtraction. You can alter the calculation order (and results) by using parentheses; Excel performs the calculation within the innermost parentheses first. For example, using parentheses, =(12+48)/24 returns 2.5 (12 is added to 48, resulting in 60; then 60 is divided by 24). Without parentheses, =12+48/24 returns 14 (48 is divided by 24, resulting in 2; then 12 is added to 2).

A good way to remember the standard order of mathematical operations is by the acronym PEMDAS—parentheses, exponents, multiplication, division, addition, subtraction. Or you can use the mnemonic "Please Excuse My Dear Aunt Sally."

Enter a Simple Formula

Use these steps to enter a simple formula:

1. Select a blank cell, and type an equal sign (=). Or select a blank cell, click in the Formula bar in the blank area to the right of the Insert Function icon, and type an equal sign.

   The equal sign displays both in the cell and in the Formula bar, as will the additional characters you type. The insertion point (where Excel expects you to type the next character) is placed to the right of the equal sign in either the cell or Formula bar, depending on where you typed it.
2. Type a value, such as **64**.
3. Type an operator, such as +.
4. Type a second value, such as **96**.
5. Complete the entry by pressing ENTER, or add additional values and operators, and then complete the entry. The result of your equation displays in the cell. (See Chapter 6 for other methods to complete an entry.)

When you're creating a formula, be careful not to click any cells that you do not want referenced in the formula. After you type the equal sign, Excel interprets any selected cell as being a cell reference in the formula.

Use Cell References

The majority of formulas use the values in other cells to produce a result—that is, the cell that contains the formula may have no value of its own, because it's derived from other cells whose values are manipulated by arithmetic operators. For example, the cell at the bottom of several values contains a formula using a function (SUM) that sums the values to produce a total, as shown next:

f_x	=SUM(F5+F6+63987+Other_Items)	
	E	F	G
5	39,876	$137,590	
6	$6,082	$23,276	
7	16,983	$63,987	
8	28,721	$109,330	
9	91,662	*$334,183*	

To use a cell reference, follow these steps:

1. Select a blank cell, and type an equal sign (=). The equal sign displays in the cell and in the Formula bar.
2. Enter a cell reference in one of the following ways:
   - Type a cell reference (for example, B4) that contains the value you want.
   - Click the cell whose value you want. A border surrounds the cell.
   - Type a named cell.
3. Type an operator.
4. Enter another cell reference or a value.
5. Complete the entry by pressing ENTER; or add more cell references, values, and operators, and then complete the entry. The result of your formula is displayed in the cell, as shown in Figure 7-2.

 Excel Online doesn't support links to *external references* in other workbooks, and you will receive error messages that indicate that the references have been disabled, as shown in Figure 7-3. Additionally, a worksheet with disabled external links will not support the use of named cells in formulas and cells containing named cells and will return an error, as shown here. Remove the external links in desktop Excel and reopen the workbook in Excel Online, and you should be able to use any named cells when creating formulas.

f_x	=F5+E7+E8+Other_Items	
	I	J
5	#VALUE!	

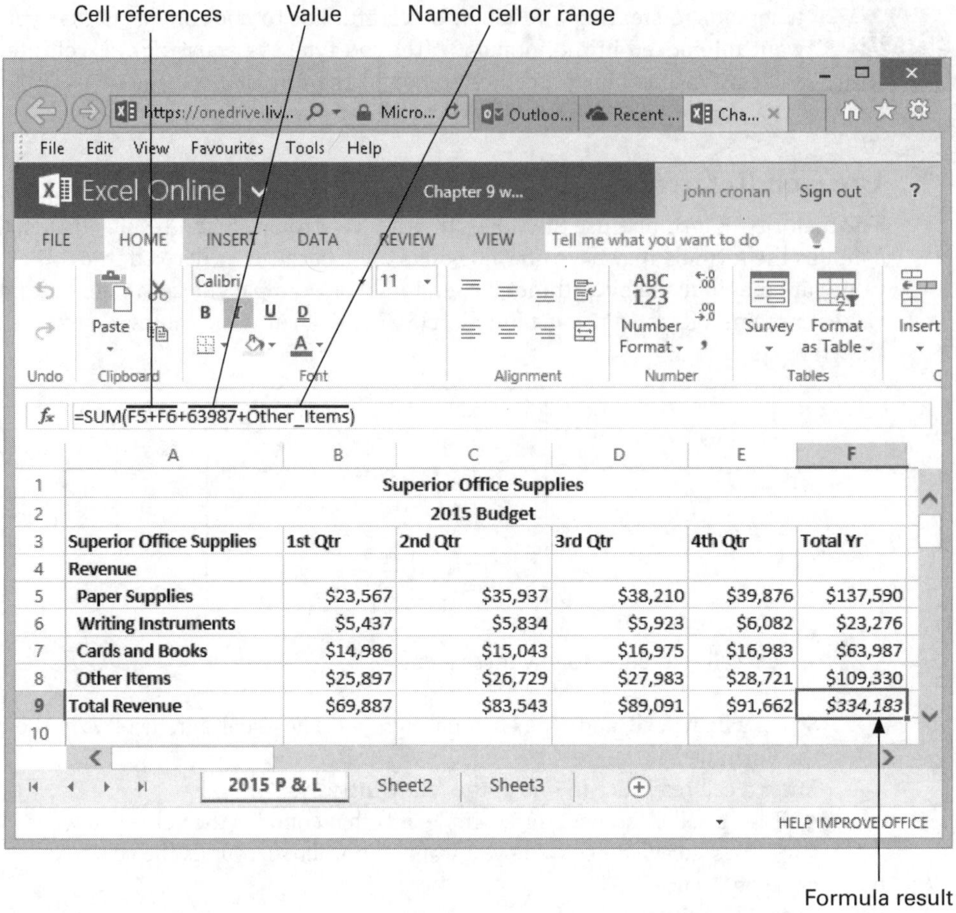

Cell references   Value   Named cell or range

FIGURE 7-2   A formula with the function SUM comprises cell references, values, and named cells.

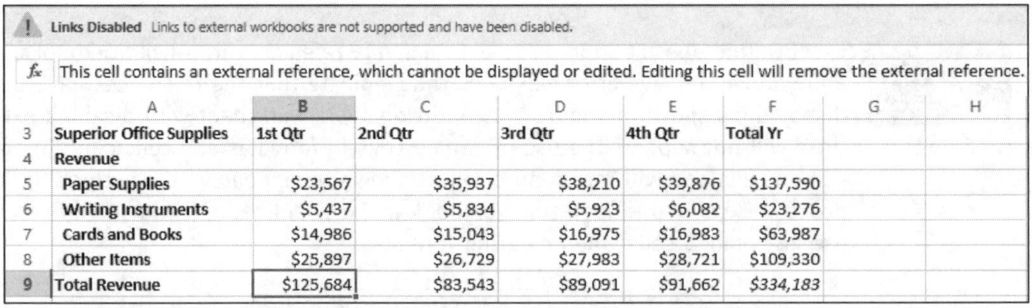

FIGURE 7-3   Unsupported external links to other workbooks can prevent using named cells in formulas.

Edit or Delete a Formula

You can easily change a formula after you have entered it.

1. Double-click the cell that contains the formula you want to change. The formula is displayed in the cell and in the Formula bar.
2. Edit the formula in one of the following ways:
   - Make changes directly in the cell or on the Formula bar.
   - Add operators and select other cells to include in the formula.
3. Complete the entry by pressing ENTER.

You can also use several techniques to get more out of working with formulas.

Replace an Entire Formula with Its Value

You can replace an entire formula with its value if you want the value to remain constant:

1. Right-click the cell that contains the formula, and click Copy.
2. In the Home tab Clipboard group, click the Paste down arrow, and click Paste Values.

Cancel or Delete a Formula

If you decide you don't want to complete a formula you're entering, press ESC.
   If you want to delete an existing formula, do one of the following:

- Select the cell that contains the formula and press DELETE.
- In the Home tab Editing group, click Clear, and then click Clear Contents.

Move Formulas

You move formulas by cutting and pasting. When you move a formula, Excel uses absolute referencing—the formula remains exactly the same as it was originally with the same cell references. (See "Change Cell References" earlier in the chapter for more information on cell referencing.) Follow these steps to move formulas:

1. Select the cell whose formula you want to move.
2. In the Home tab Clipboard group, click Cut or press CTRL-X.
   Alternatively, right-click the cell whose formula you want to move and click Cut.

3. Select the cell where you want to move the formula.
4. In the Home tab Clipboard group, click Paste or press CTRL-V. Alternatively, right-click the cell where you want to move the formula and click Paste.

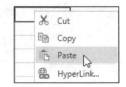

Copy Formulas

When you copy formulas, relative referencing is applied. Therefore, cell referencing in a formula will change when you copy the formula, unless you have made a reference absolute. If you do not get the results you expect, click Undo in the Home tab Undo group, and change the cell references before you copy again.

Copy Formulas into Adjacent Cells

Use these steps to copy formulas into adjacent cells:

1. Select the cell whose formula you want to copy.
2. Point at the fill handle in the lower-right corner of the cell, and drag over the cells where you want the formula copied.

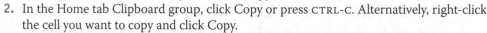

15	Medicare	$242	$249
16	Total Expenses	$10,874	
17			

Copy Formulas into Nonadjacent Cells

Use these steps to copy formulas into nonadjacent cells:

1. Select the cell whose formula you want to copy.
2. In the Home tab Clipboard group, click Copy or press CTRL-C. Alternatively, right-click the cell you want to copy and click Copy.
3. Copy formatting along with the formula by selecting the destination cell. Then, in the Home tab Clipboard group, click Paste.

If you want to copy just the formula without the formatting, select the destination cell. Then, in the Home tab Clipboard group, click the Paste down arrow and click Paste Formulas.

Recalculate Formulas

By default, Excel automatically recalculates formulas in the workbook affected by changes to a value, to the formula itself, or to a changed referenced cell, and when the workbook is saved. You also can recalculate more frequently by doing one of the following:

- Press F9.
- In the Data tab Calculation group, click Calculate Workbook.

Use Worksheet References in Formulas

You can *link* data using cell references to worksheets other than the one you are currently working in (but in the same workbook). For example, if you are building a departmental budget, you could link to each division's budget workbook and have any changes made to formulas in those workbooks be applied automatically to your total budget workbook. Changes made to the references in the *source* worksheet are automatically updated in the *destination* worksheet when the data is entered. Here's how to do this:

1. In the destination worksheet, create the formula or open an existing formula.
2. Place the insertion point in the formula where you want to insert the external reference.
3. Type the source address using the form: '*Sheet Name*'/*Reference Identifier*(!)/*Cell Address or Range or Name*. For example, to sum data from the B4 cell in a source worksheet named QTR1 Revenue to an existing range in a destination worksheet, the formula in the destination worksheet would be

   =SUM(B5:B8, 'QTR1 Revenue'!B4)

   as shown in Figure 7-4.
4. Press ENTER to complete the entry.

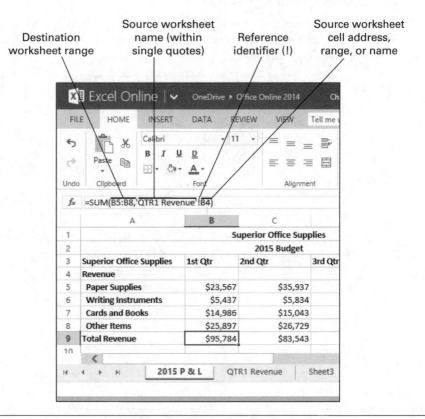

FIGURE 7-4   A reference in a formula to another sheet in the workbook comprises several components.

Use Functions

Functions are prewritten formulas that you can use to perform specific tasks. They can be as simple as =PI(), which returns 3.14159265358979, the value of the constant pi; or they can be as complex as =PPMT(rate,per,nper,pv,fv,type), which returns a payment on an investment principal.

A function comprises three components:

- **Formula identifier**, the equal sign (=), is required when a function is at the beginning of the formula.
- **Function name** identifies the function, and typically is a two- to five-character uppercase abbreviation.
- **Arguments** are the values acted upon by functions to derive a result. They can be numbers, cell references, constants, logical (True or False) values, or a formula. Arguments are separated by commas and enclosed in parentheses. A function can include up to 255 arguments.

Use Functions Quickly

You can view the results of several popular functions by selecting a range. By default, the average, count, and sum of the selected cells are shown on the right of the status bar at the bottom of the Excel window.

	4th Qtr	Total Yr		
$38,210	$39,876	$137,590		#V/
$5,923	$6,082	$23,276		
$16,975	$16,983	$63,987		
$27,983	$28,721	$109,330		

AVERAGE: $22,916   COUNT: 4   SUM: $91,662   ▾   HELP IMPROVE OFFICE

You can change which function results are displayed on the status bar by clicking the Customize Status Bar down arrow and selecting the results you want.

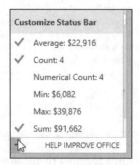

Customize Status Bar

✓ Average: $22,916
✓ Count: 4
   Numerical Count: 4
   Min: $6,082
   Max: $39,876
✓ Sum: $91,662
   HELP IMPROVE OFFICE

Enter a Function

Enter functions on a worksheet by typing, as described earlier in this chapter for formulas, a combination of typing and selecting cell references whose values you want to include in the function. In addition, you can search for and choose functions from Excel's library of built-in functions.

 Tip You do not need to type the closing parenthesis; Excel will add it for you when you complete the entry. However, it is good practice to include a closing parenthesis for each opening parenthesis. This is especially true if you use complex, nested functions that include other functions as arguments. (You may nest up to 64 levels.)

Type a Function

To type a function in a cell on the worksheet, follow these steps:

1. Select a blank cell, and type an equal sign (=). The equal sign displays in the cell and the Formula bar.
2. Start typing the function name, such as AVERAGE, MAX, or PMT. As you start typing, functions with related spellings are displayed. Click any to see a description of the function, as shown in Figure 7-5.

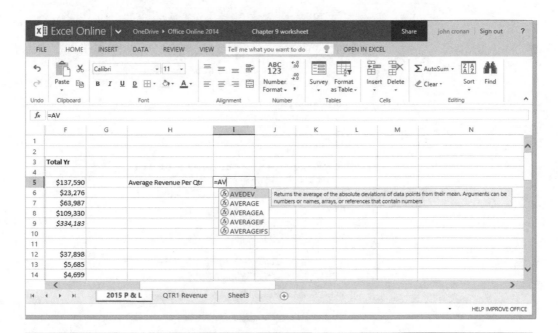

FIGURE 7-5 As you type, Excel's AutoComplete provides focused access to its function library and information about selected functions.

3. Double-click the function you want. The function name and open parenthesis are entered for you. Excel displays a tooltip showing arguments and proper syntax for the function.

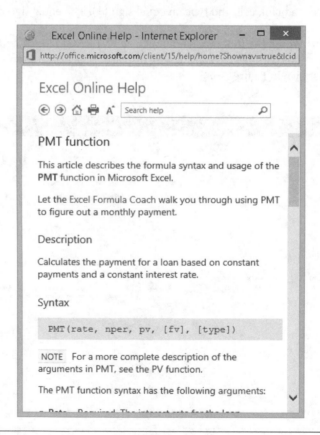

4. Depending on the function, for each argument, do none, one, or both of the following:
   - Type the argument.
   - Select a cell reference.
5. Type a comma to separate arguments, and repeat steps 4 and 5 as necessary.
6. Press ENTER to complete the entry (the closing parenthesis is automatically added for you). A value will be returned. (If a *#code* is displayed in the cell or a message box displays, they indicate you made an error. Click the cell that contains the function and review the syntax to ensure you have the correct number and type of arguments.)

Tip If you need more information regarding a function or its arguments, click the function name in the tooltip at step 3. An Excel Online Help page opens that describes the function, as shown in Figure 7-6.

FIGURE 7-6 Assistance on functions is available from Excel Online Help.

Insert a Function

You can find the function you want using the Insert Function dialog box.

1. Select a blank cell.

 2. Click the Insert Function button on the Formula bar, or press SHIFT-F3. The Insert Function dialog box appears, as shown here:

3. In the Pick A Category drop-down list, select a category.
4. Select the function you want from the Pick A Function list box. Its arguments and syntax are shown, as well as a description of what the function returns.
5. Enter values for the arguments by typing or clicking cell references, typing separators such as commas and parentheses as the function syntax calls for. The formula on the worksheet is built as you enter each argument.
6. Click OK to complete the entry.

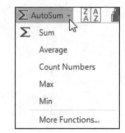

Tip Using the AutoSum option, you can apply common functions to selected cells, such as averaging and getting a count. In the Home tab Editing group, click the AutoSum down arrow, and click the function you want; or click More Functions to open the Insert Function dialog box and access the full function library.

Enter a Sum in Columns or Rows Quickly

AutoSum uses the SUM function to add contiguous numbers quickly. To enter a sum quickly, select a contiguous column or row of cells, and then click AutoSum in the Home tab Editing group. The sum is entered in the first blank cell at either the bottom of a column of cells or to the right of a row of cells.

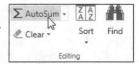

Work with Tables

Excel enables you to work with data in *tables*. Tables, like databases, consist of columns of similar data—the names and related information for all the salespeople in a company, for example. Each salesperson covers a certain region, so this table would also need a Territory column. Each salesperson has a cell phone number, each has projected sales targets and actual sales, and so forth. You could say each salesperson has a collection of information pertaining just to him or her. In an Excel table, each row in the worksheet contains this collection of unique data—unique in the sense that although two or more salespeople might call Washington their territory, as shown next, each row contains data for only one salesperson.

	A	B	C	D	E
1	Last Name	First Name	Territory	Qtr Sales	Phone
2	Edwards	George	Alaska	$8,425.00	425-555-1234
3	Thomas	Bob	Washington	$14,235.00	425-5554321
4	Wong	Sue	Oregon	$18,439.00	425-555-5678
5	Garcia	Maria	Idaho	$9,253.00	425-555-8765
6	Smith	John	Washington	$21,987.00	425-555-0908
7	Brown	Sally	Washington	$13,654.00	425-555-4567

When you work with cells in or adjacent to a table, Excel automatically "comes to the table" with several tools and features to help you avoid mouse clicks and keystrokes, and this basically make your work in tables easier, faster, and more efficient.

In the days before Microsoft had a database product, such as Access or SQL (Structured Query Language) Server, an Excel *list* provided basic database functions. From its database roots, you may see database terms used when referring to tables—for example, in database terminology, columns are called *fields*, rows are called *records*, and the table itself, though often called a table, may also be called a *datasheet*. So you can call a series of rows of related data that is organized into categories a table, a list, a datasheet, or even (sometimes) a database.

You can create tables easily from scratch or by selecting an existing range of data. Moreover, once Excel recognizes data is within a table, it makes assumptions that help you to view, enter, filter, and use the data in calculations.

Insert a Table

You can create a blank table and then enter data, or you can select a range of pre-existing data and convert the range to a table.

 Once a range is converted to a table it cannot be changed back to a range.

Insert a Blank Table

Use these steps to insert a blank table:

1. On the worksheet where you want to create a table, drag to create a range comprising the number of columns and rows you think you need for your data.

Note that you can expand a table by entering more data in the bottom row to create additional rows or by adding data in the column to the right of the table to add a column.

2. Do one of the following:
   - In the Insert tab Tables group, click Table.
   - In the Home tab Tables group, click the Format As Table button.

3. In either case, the Create Table dialog box opens. Verify that the displayed range defines your table, and select My Table Has Headers if your table will contain column headers.

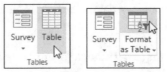

4. Click OK. The table is created (see Figure 7-7) with placeholder column headers that you can edit to fit your data, alternating row colors for better data differentiation, and an AutoFilter down arrow to access easy filtering and sorting of data (see "Use AutoFilter" later in the chapter for information on using filters).

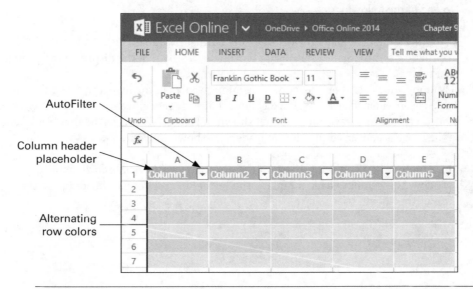

FIGURE 7-7 A new table makes functional and visual tools immediately available to you.

Quickly create a table by selecting a range and pressing CTRL-L. Select whether the first row contains column headers, and click OK.

Create a Table from Existing Data

Before you designate a range of data to be a table, you might want to consider reorganizing your data to work better with table features.

- **Column headers** (or *labels*) should be formatted differently from the data so that Excel can more easily differentiate one from the other. All data in a column should be similar. Avoid mixing dates and other number formats with text.
- **Clean up the data range** by eliminating any blank rows or columns within the range and removing extra spaces in cells.
- **Display all data** by showing any rows or columns you might have hidden. Hidden data can be inadvertently deleted (see Chapter 8 to view hidden data).
- **Place values to be totaled** in the rightmost column. Excel's Total Row feature creates a total row, which you can toggle off or on, when it recognizes data that can be summed in the last column.

 Use the Borders button in the Home tab Font group to add a border that separates column headers from data instead of spacing or other separation techniques. ⊞

To create a table from existing data, follow these steps:

1. Select the data you want to be included within a table.
2. Do one of the following:
   - In the Insert tab Tables group, click Table.
   - In the Home tab Tables groups, click the Format As Table button.
   In either case, the Create Table dialog box opens. Verify that the displayed range defines your table.
3. Assuming your data is organized with column headers in the first row, select the My Table Has Headers check box, if Excel doesn't already recognize them. Click OK. The table is created in a way similar to that shown in Figure 7-7, except the first row of data in the range is converted to column headers, as shown in Figure 7-8.

 In a table, when you scroll through data beyond what's visible in the sheet window, the column headers replace the lettered Excel column headings at the top of the sheet.

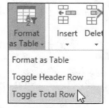

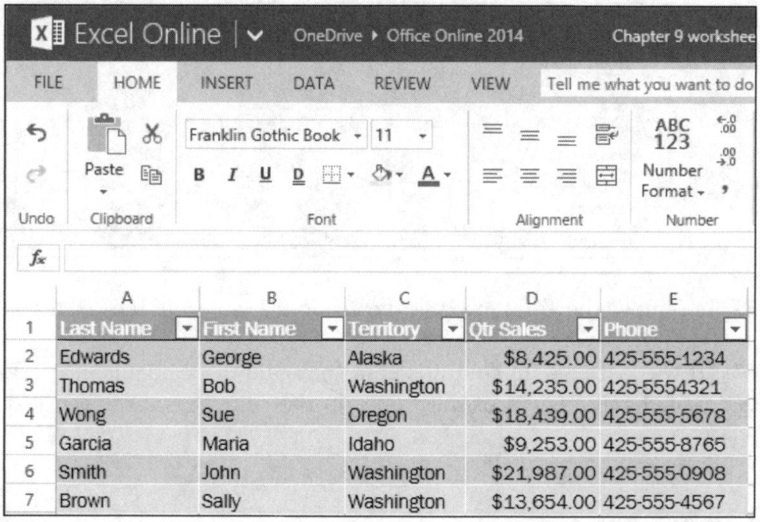

FIGURE 7-8   A table created from existing data can include the first row of headers.

Change Rows and Columns in a Table

Tables are easily resized by adding rows and columns:

- To add rows to the end of the table, type in an empty row that is adjacent to the end of the table. The table will "annex" the row, unless the last row is empty or the last row is a total row.
- To add columns to the sides of a table, type in an empty column that is adjacent to the right side of the table. The table will "annex" the column.

Add a Total Row

Excel provides a nifty feature that sums the last column in a table and automatically creates a Total row at the bottom of the table. The Total row lets you perform other calculations on any of the columns in the table.

1. Select a cell in the table.
2. In the Home tab Tables group, click the Format As Table down arrow, and click Toggle Total Row. The rightmost column is summed within a new row, with the word "Total" in the leftmost cell, as shown here:

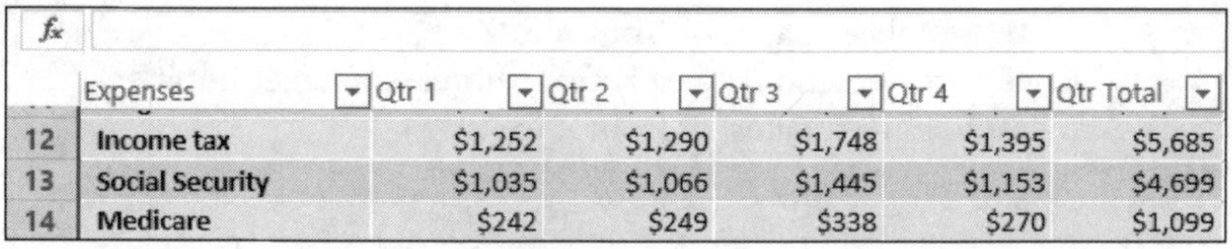

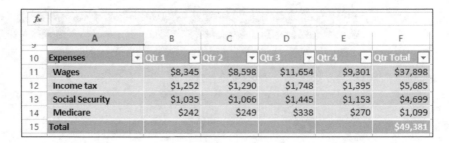

	A	B	C	D	E	F
10	**Expenses** ▾	Qtr 1 ▾	Qtr 2 ▾	Qtr 3 ▾	Qtr 4 ▾	Qtr Total ▾
11	**Wages**	$8,345	$8,598	$11,654	$9,301	$37,898
12	**Income tax**	$1,252	$1,290	$1,748	$1,395	$5,685
13	**Social Security**	$1,035	$1,066	$1,445	$1,153	$4,699
14	**Medicare**	$242	$249	$338	$270	$1,099
15	**Total**					$49,381

3. To remove the Total row, select a cell in the table and repeat step 2.

Note If the last column contains data that cannot be summed, the Total row is still added and a count of the values in the column is displayed instead of a sum.

Organize Data

Data in a worksheet is often entered in a manner that doesn't lend itself well to being viewed or to being able to find specific data that you want. Excel provides several tools to assist you in organizing your data without permanently changing the overall structure of the worksheet. You can sort data on any column in ascending or descending order, filter data in tables to view just the information you want to see, and add more sheets to separate categories of data.

Perform an Ascending/Descending Sort

You can sort data based on ascending or descending order according to the values in the column. Excel sorts numbers "smallest to largest" and dates "oldest to newest," considered "ascending," as well as their reverse.

Tip You can sort data anywhere on a worksheet. However, when sorting outside of a table, you have to be careful to correctly select the data that you want sorted, or you run the risk that related data becomes disassociated (data in one column might change, while the data in the rest of the columns remains the same).

To sort data, follow these steps:

1. Click a cell in the column of a range or table that you want to sort.
2. In the Home tab Editing group, click Sort, and then do one of the following:
   - Click Sort Ascending to sort from smaller to larger numbers, newest to oldest dates, or from A to Z.
   - Click Sort Descending to sort from larger to smaller numbers, oldest to newest dates, or from Z to A.

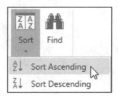

Sorting in Excel is determined by a specified *sort order*. For example, numbers in an ascending sort are sorted before letters; combined number and letter (*alphanumeric*) values are sorted next; logical values with False, and then logical values with True; then error values; and finally, any blanks.

Use AutoFilter

Filtering data allows you to hide potentially thousands of rows (records) of data that you don't need at the moment so that only those rows of data that you want to see are displayed. AutoFilter down arrows are added to column headers when you create a table (see Figures 7-8 and 7-9). The quickest and easiest way to filter data is to have Excel add AutoFilter to your column headings.

1. Click a cell in the range or table where you want to filter data.
2. Click the AutoFilter down arrow in the heading of the column that contains the values to which you want to apply a filter.
3. Decide what you want to filter from the menu.
   - Click *Number/Text/Date* Filter to filter based on the type of data in the column using filter criteria, as shown in Figure 7-9.
   - Click Filter to select from all values in the column to include or exclude from the filter, as shown Figure 7-10.

Follow the appropriate steps in the following sections to create the filter you want.

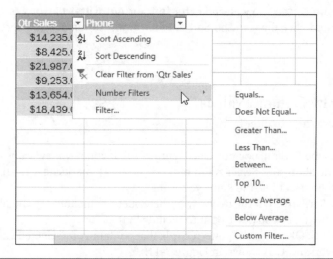

FIGURE 7-9   **Filtering numeric data provides several tuned options to focus quickly on specific data.**

FIGURE 7-10   You can select to view only the rows in a column that match the values you choose.

 Sorting options are also available on the AutoFilter menu. In fact, columns that are sorted show an indicator in their AutoFilter buttons (select a sorted column, and click Clear in the Sort & Filter group to remove the sort indicator).

Filter by Column Values

Use these steps to filter by column values:

1. In the Filter dialog box (see Figure 7-10), if you have few values you want to include in the filter, click Select All to remove the check marks next to all values in the column, and then select just the items you want.
    Alternatively, if the majority of the values are included in the filter, simply uncheck the few values you don't want to include in the filter.
2. Click OK. Only the rows/records that contain your selected values are displayed on the worksheet, as shown in Figure 7-11.

Filter by Empty Cells

The Blanks option is displayed only if the column has at least one blank cell.
    To filter by empty cells, follow these steps:

...that contain the filtering values
(Washington and Oregon) display
after applying a filter.   Filter indicator

Only the records
(while maintaining
their original row
numbers)...

	A	B	C	D	E
1	Last Name ▼	First Name ▾	Territory ▾	Qtr Sales ▼	Phone ▼
2	Thomas	Bob	Washington	$14,235.00	425-555-4321
4	Smith	John	Washington	$21,987.00	
6	Brown	Sally	Washington	$13,654.00	425-555-4567
7	Wong	Sue	Oregon	$18,439.00	425-555-5678

FIGURE 7-11   **Filtering displays only the records that contain a value or match a criteria.**

1. In the Filter dialog box (see Figure 7-10), click Select All to remove the check marks next to all values in the column.
2. Select (Blanks) at the bottom of the Select Item list. Then click OK.

Filter

Select item:

☐ (Select All)
☐ 425-555-4321
☐ 425-555-4567
☐ 425-555-5678
☑ (Blanks)

Filter by Numeric Values

Excel provides several "quick" criteria you can choose from to filter your data quickly.

1. On the Filter menu, click Number Filters. A list of criteria options is displayed:

Equals...

Does Not Equal...

Greater Than...

Less Than...

Between...

Top 10...

Above Average

Below Average

Custom Filter...

2. Click the comparison you want to filter by. Then type or select one or more values in the Custom Filter dialog and click OK. (Clicking Above Average or Below Average immediately performs the filter; clicking Top 10 opens a dialog box, where you can filter for top or bottom values or percentages.)

Custom Filter   ✕

Show items where: **Qtr Sales**

| is between ▼ | 10000 | and | 15000 |

OK   Cancel

You can also filter columns that contain text and dates instead of numeric values. These filters have their own set of quick filter criteria you can choose from.

Create a Custom Filter

If the comparisons on the particular filter you choose don't offer what you are trying to achieve with your filter, you can access the Custom Filter dialog box directly and select from an expanded list of comparison filters:

1. On the Filter menu, click Number Filters (or Text Filters or Date Filters depending on the data), and then click Custom Filter.
2. In the Custom Filter dialog box, click the Show Items Where: *columnname* down arrow and click the comparison you want.
3. If applicable, type the criteria that is required in the text boxes to the right. Click OK.

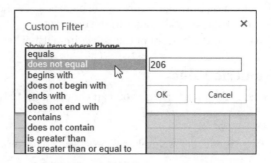

Remove a Filter from a Column

Use these steps to remove a filter from a column:

 1. Click the AutoFilter button next to the column heading.
2. Click Clear Filter From '*columnname*'.

Use Worksheets to Organize Data

To organize your workbook better, you can add worksheets to separate categories of data (by default, new workbooks in Excel Online start with one sheet). For example, you could create four quarters of sales information, each on its own sheet, and then create a fifth summary sheet. Excel provides several tools at the bottom of the Excel window that you can use to modify the number and identification of worksheets in a workbook.

Add a Worksheet

To add a worksheet, click the New Sheet button (the plus sign) to the right of the current worksheet(s). A new worksheet is added to the right of any current tabs.

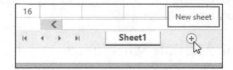

Delete a Worksheet

To delete a worksheet, right-click the worksheet tab of the worksheet you want to delete, and click Delete from the context menu.

Move a Worksheet

You can move worksheets within a workbook by dragging a worksheet's tab or by reordering them.

- To move a worksheet, drag the worksheet tab to the position on the worksheet bar where you want it to appear. A small downward triangle shows where it will be placed.

- To reorder your sheets, right-click the sheet you want to move, click Reorder on the context menu, and in the Move Selected Sheet dialog box, select which sheet you want to its right (or you can place it in the rightmost position—at the end). Click OK.

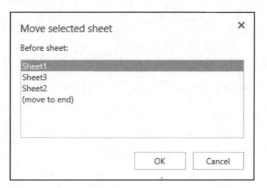

Rename a Worksheet

To rename a worksheet, right-click the worksheet tab of the worksheet you want to rename, and click Rename on the context menu. Type a new worksheet name, and press ENTER.

Hide Sheets

To hide a sheet, right-click the worksheet tab of the worksheet you want to hide, and click Hide. The sheet is removed from the status bar.

To unhide a sheet, right-click any sheet and click Unhide. In the Unhide dialog box, select the sheet you want to reappear, and click OK.

Move Through Multiple Worksheets

To move through worksheets, click a sheet tab to select the one you want to use. If there are more sheets than can be shown, you can use the navigation buttons on the left end of the worksheet bar to move from worksheet to worksheet.

When you click the left and right arrows at the left end of the worksheet bar, you move one sheet in the direction of the arrow. Clicking the arrows with a vertical line to the left and right of the arrows moves the sheets to their beginning or end, respectively.

8

Creating a Presentation with PowerPoint Online

HOW TO...

- Create slide presentations
- Work with PowerPoint themes, layouts, and templates
- Add content to slides
- Insert art and graphics
- Navigate and manipulate slides
- Add animations and transitions to slides

In this chapter, you are introduced to PowerPoint Online, the slide presentation program available with Microsoft Office Online. PowerPoint Online gives you a selection of tools, templates, themes, and designs from which to choose. If you have used other versions of PowerPoint, you will find many of your favorite tools available in the online version.

You may find what you need in the prepackaged themes and templates that are designed with specific presentation types in mind (for instance, an academic or business presentation, or a presentation fashioned for *your* industry). You may find that one of your previous presentations has what you need, so you can simply borrow slides or design elements from past successful efforts. Sometimes, however, nothing in your presentation library or in the PowerPoint templates can fill your particular requirements. In this case, you can create your own template from scratch or with Office-wide themes and the styling assistance of PowerPoint. This chapter looks at how to organize and manage your slides by creating and working with your content.

Begin to Use PowerPoint

As with Word and Excel, you can learn the most about PowerPoint by opening the program and exploring.

In this chapter, we'll use "PowerPoint" to refer to "PowerPoint Online" unless it is necessary to distinguish which version is being discussed. We'll use "PowerPoint desktop" to refer to any version of PowerPoint that is installed on any device, and not online.

Start PowerPoint

Start PowerPoint in one of two ways:

- Open your browser, type **office.com**, press ENTER, and click the PowerPoint Online icon.
- In the browser window, type **onedrive.com**, sign in if asked, click the down arrow to the right of OneDrive, and click the PowerPoint Online icon to open PowerPoint.

When you first open PowerPoint, you'll see the Let's Get Started banner. From here, you can open a new blank presentation, browse templates, or open recent documents on OneDrive. We'll look at all three options in this chapter.

 To bypass the Let's Get Started banner when you start PowerPoint, open an existing document by opening OneDrive, locating, and clicking a PowerPoint document. PowerPoint will open and display the document. From here, you can work on the document or open another one.

Begin with a New Blank Slide

In the Let's Get Started banner, click New Blank Presentation. PowerPoint will open with a blank title slide into which you can start typing your presentation immediately. Figure 8-1 shows the title slide.

Tabs contain the categories of editing tools. When you open a tab, you see the tools associated with that tab. When an object is highlighted in the presentation pane, a new tab associated with that object is displayed—such as the selected text box and its associated Format tab shown in Figure 8-1. The ribbon (discussed in Chapter 1) contains the tools you will use to edit a presentation, organized within groups. In the presentation pane, you will see an entire slide. This is where you do most of your work while creating the slide contents. You can manage your slides from the slides pane—such as moving, duplicating, and adding new slides. In the Notes pane, you add notes about each slide so that collaborators can read information about the slide. The status bar enables you to track which slide you're working on; to add comments to Microsoft; to expand the Notes pane; and to alter your view between reading slides, editing slides, and running a slide show.

 Your ribbon options will vary depending on the size of your window. Windows that are not maximized in size display abbreviated options, such as the Styles and Editing groups on the right end of the ribbon.

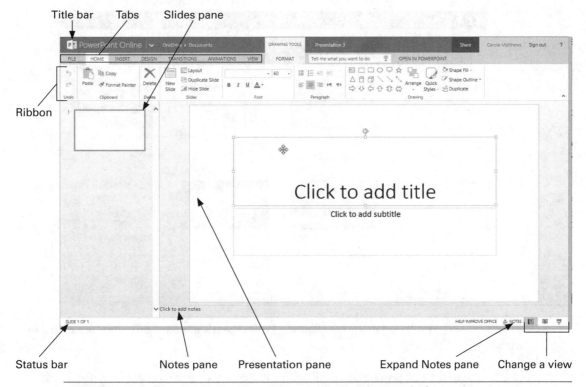

FIGURE 8-1   When you start PowerPoint, a blank slide is ready for you to create a presentation immediately.

Begin with Templates

PowerPoint contains many templates in the online version to help you design your presentation with preset themes and layouts. (See "Understand Themes, Layouts, and Templates" later in the chapter to get a clearer understanding of how the three work together to distinguish a slide.) Templates contain not only the blank title slide, but also a number of other slides that you may need in your total presentation. Templates are organized by category to facilitate your search. For instance, if you are looking for a brochure, you'll find a selection of preset templates that you can use and modify as you need for your own use.

To use a template, follow these steps:

1. On the Let's Get Started banner, click Browse Templates. You'll see the Templates for PowerPoint window, shown in Figure 8-2.
2. On the left are several suggested categories. Tap or click the category name, such as Brochures, to open another window displaying thumbnails.
3. Click the thumbnail of the template you like. When the selected template opens, it may show variants below the displayed template.
4. When you see what you want, click Open In PowerPoint Online. Then click Continue to save the presentation to OneDrive.

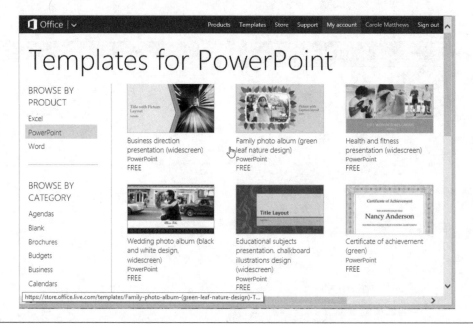

FIGURE 8-2 You'll find many templates in PowerPoint's standard offerings, organized by category.

A complete blank presentation will open with layouts of several slides included in the presentation, as shown in Figure 8-3. You can use or delete any of these slides as needed. This presentation is now available to you as an option in your list of existing documents.

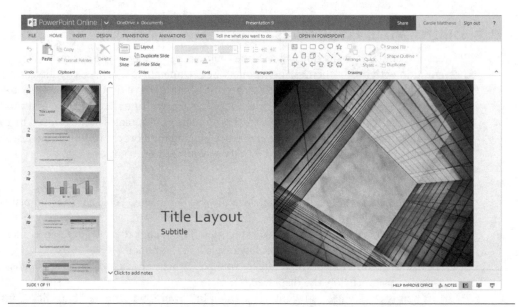

FIGURE 8-3 After choosing a template, you start with several preset slides with a given theme and layout.

When you create a new slideshow using a template, PowerPoint gives your presentation file a standard name, such as "Presentation 9." If you want to rename it, save it to your computer with a different name. Then open it in PowerPoint Online.

Open an Existing Presentation

If you've already created a presentation, you can edit or modify it to create a new presentation. Follow these steps:

1. On the Let's Get Started banner, click Recent Documents on OneDrive. You'll see a list of all your recently used documents.
2. Click the document you want—make sure you're clicking a PowerPoint document, since *all* your recent documents are shown here. The presentation will open in the Reading View (see "Explore PowerPoint Online Views" later in the chapter) which contains a different set of tabs.

3. Click Edit Presentation | Edit In PowerPoint Online. The PowerPoint presentation will open in the Editing View (see "Explore PowerPoint Online Views" later in the chapter) with the editing-enabled set of tabs (shown earlier in Figure 8-1).

 As good as PowerPoint's automatic saving is, it is a great idea to save your presentation frequently (at least a couple of times an hour). Doing this can save you the frustration of working several hours on a slide show only to lose your work. Chapter 3 discussed how to save a document.

Create a Presentation

You can find a theme and begin creating your presentation in one of three ways:

- Use a standard template that defines the design and layout of a slide (as described in the section "Begin with Templates").
- Use an existing presentation (as described in "Open an Existing Presentation") and then modify it.
- Start from scratch and create your own template.

To understand how the parts of a presentation work together, you must first understand the differences between themes, layouts, and templates.

Understand Themes, Layouts, and Templates

Themes in PowerPoint lend presentations color and design coordination. PowerPoint uses themes to give your presentation a unified and professional look. Themes provide background color and design, predefined fonts, and other elements that hold a presentation together. Design elements contain fonts, font sizes, border weight, use of bold and italics, design shapes—for example, the document shown in Figure 8-3 shows a blue theme with particular fonts and other elements already chosen. More than 20 themes are available in the Design tab Themes group. After you have selected a theme, you can find additional choices from the Variants group. This chapter and Chapter 9 explain how you can change a theme or customize your presentation for almost unlimited variations of how your presentation looks.

Layouts define where the objects of a slide (such as titles, text, spreadsheets or diagrams, pictures, or headings and footers) will be placed and formatted. Objects are positioned on a slide using *placeholders* that identify the specific object being inserted (a text placeholder versus a picture placeholder, for instance). When you insert a new slide into a given theme, the slide takes on the colors and design elements of the presentation's theme, with the chosen layout's placeholders positioned according to the layout's purpose.

 To search online for additional templates (multiple blank slides containing both themes and layouts), click the More On Office.com link after clicking File | New. Microsoft calls these online "templates" and the Design tab options "themes." It becomes confusing which is which. Keep in mind the following: Templates contain both layouts and themes. Themes are aspects defining and coordinating color and design elements. Layouts define the positioning of placeholders, thereby contributing to the purpose of a slide.

Find a Theme

Once you have defined the overall theme, it is a simple task to add slides with the appropriate layout for the data you want to present. You can select a theme from the predefined gallery in the Design tab and then select a variant available with that theme.

After you click the OneDrive down-arrow, select PowerPoint Online, and select New Blank Presentation in the Let's Get Started options, your next task is to find a theme. Here are two ways you can find and use one of PowerPoint's standard themes:

- If you are in PowerPoint, click File | New to see a selection of available themes. Click one and it will open in a blank presentation with a single slide.
- In the PowerPoint window, click the Design tab and from the Themes group, select the theme you want to use by clicking its thumbnail. Click the More Themes down-arrow at the lower right of the thumbnail gallery to see the whole list of themes.

Once you have chosen a theme, you will also see variants on the theme in the Design tab Variants group. Click a variant to use it. At this point you can begin to add slides and content to an actual presentation.

When you select a theme or a variant, the color and design elements (such as fonts, font size, use of bold and italic, design shapes, and so on) will apply to all slides in the presentation, not just the selected slides.

Add New Slides and Layouts

After you have selected a theme, the presentation will contain at least one new blank slide, the title slide. Then you can add new slides with different layouts:

1. On the title slide, click "Click To Add Title" and enter the title of your presentation. If you want to add a subtitle, click "Click To Add Subtitle" and type a subtitle.
2. To add a new blank slide with another layout but the same theme, do one of the following:
   - From the Home tab Slides group, click New Slide. A dialog box lists the available layouts (see Figure 8-4). Click the one you want and click Add Slide.
   - To add a new slide with another layout, click Insert tab | New Slide. Then double-click the layout you want.
3. To change the layout of a slide, from the Home tab Slides group, click Layout to open a list of layout options. Click a layout and then click Change Layout to replace the layout on the current slide with the selected one.
4. To duplicate, hide, and delete slides, see "Navigate and Manipulate Slides" later in the chapter.
5. Repeat steps 2 and 3 for as many slides as you have in your presentation.
6. The presentation is saved automatically to OneDrive, but you can save a copy to the Downloads folder on your computer by clicking File | Save As | Download | Save.

To delete a slide from the slides pane, click the thumbnail slide to select it and press DELETE. You can also right-click the thumbnail slide and click Delete Slide from the context menu.

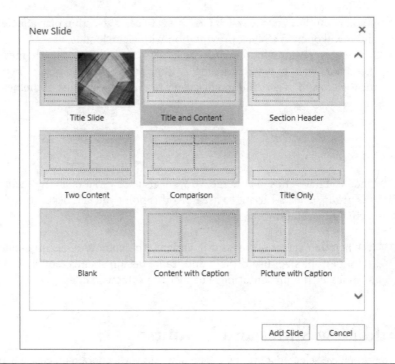

FIGURE 8-4 When you insert a new slide, you also select the layout you want.

Add Content to a Slide

PowerPoint offers many elements to help you present and highlight information in your presentations. For instance, regardless of whether you begin with a blank slide or one with a template, you can add or change layouts, color schemes, fonts, graphics, charts, and text. Following is an overview of the procedures for adding content to a slide.

Work with Text

You add text to placeholders (such as the "Title Layout" placeholder on the title slide shown in Figure 8-3), in text boxes, or inside some shapes. (Chapter 9 discusses working with text in detail.) To add text, click a placeholder, inside a text box, or within a shape and begin to type.

To modify text attributes, highlight the text by dragging over it. In the text toolbar, shown next, select changes.

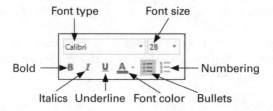

Alternatively, from the Home tab, make selections from the Font group. The Paragraph group in the Home tab contains additional text settings. (See Chapter 9 for additional information about using text.)

Add or Change Color Schemes

Ask yourself what color schemes you want to use. Do you want to use particular company colors to match other company literature, or are there specific colors you don't want to use? You can easily change the color theme. See "Find a Theme" for details.

 When you change the color of a slide, all slides will be affected.

Select an Animations or Transitions Scheme

Animation adds action to a slide, such as objects that appear in the presentation according to your directions. For instance, perhaps you want listed text to appear on the slide one line at a time in a particular way—for example, flying in from the top. You can control the timing of what the viewer sees, so that information appears on cue. Then introduce new objects with a click of your mouse.

Transitions control how one slide advances to the next, adding interest to the presentation. Perhaps you'd like the new slide to fade in over the current slide.

You can add animations and transitions in a number of ways.

To display animated text on your slide, follow these steps:

1. Open the Animations tab.
2. Highlight the text or graphic you want to be animated.
3. From the Animations group, click the animation scheme you want.
4. See "Add Animations and Transitions to Slides" later in the chapter for additional details.

To control the transition of one slide to the next, follow these steps:

1. With a slide open, click the Transitions tab.
2. Click the slide in the slides pane that will be displayed with the transition effect, and then click the transition effect in the Transitions group.
3. See "Add Animations and Transitions to Slides" later in the chapter for additional details.

Insert Art and Graphics

You can add interest by adding pictures, clipart, or graphics to a presentation. For instance, you can make a presentation more professional looking by formatting your bulleted or numbered lists with SmartArt graphics.

1. With a slide open, click the Insert tab, and in the Illustrations group, click the button for the art or graphic object you want to insert. The object will be inserted in its own placeholder.
2. Drag the inserted object where you want it on the current slide.

3. Resize the object as needed by selecting it and dragging its handles, as shown next.

Switch Between PowerPoint Online and Desktop PowerPoint

Because the functions within PowerPoint Online are limited, you may want to work with the Desktop PowerPoint version on occasion. When you are using PowerPoint Online, you may find you need a feature only available in the desktop version.

 If you use a feature in the desktop version that is unavailable in the online version, it will still appear in the online version's presentation and will work correctly when the slide show is activated. But you will not be able to see it work in the Editing or Reading Views, and you won't be able to edit the item. Nevertheless, switching between the two versions to access the full capabilities of the desktop version is a powerful tool.

You can easily switch to the desktop version, insert a feature into the presentation, and switch back to the online version. Follow these steps:

1. In your online presentation, click the Open In PowerPoint button located to the right of the tabs. If a dialog box asks if it is OK for PowerPoint to open on your computer, click Allow. If requested, sign in to your Microsoft account.

2. Make changes and additions as needed.
3. When you are ready to return to the online version, save your presentation to OneDrive. (If you haven't changed the name since opening the presentation, simply save it and it will save to OneDrive.)
4. Close the desktop version and return to PowerPoint Online in your browser. The changes will appear in your online version.

Explore PowerPoint Online Views

Online PowerPoint offers views that help you edit, read, or display your presentation. Depending on your task, you can use the view you need. You can access views in two ways:

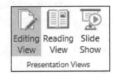

- In the View tab Presentation Views group, click the view you want.
- At the lower-right corner of the status bar, click the icon for the view you want.

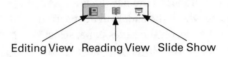

Editing View   Reading View   Slide Show

Here is what each view offers:

- **Editing View**   Displays the standard toolbar plus the slides pane, so that you can easily find and manipulate the slides you want. This is the default view.
- **Reading View**   Displays the document pane only without the slides pane. Tabs allow you to switch to the Editing View, to share with others, to start the slide show, or to view and add comments. Although you can easily change the presentation, editing itself is not available on this view.
- **Slide Show**   Starts the slide show so you can see the presentation as it is currently being developed.

Navigate and Manipulate Slides

As you work with slides, you'll find your way around your presentation to manipulate the slides, both individually and globally. This section addresses how to insert and delete slides, display slides in a variety of ways, and move and duplicate slides.

Move to the Next or Previous Slide

You can use the keyboard to move to the next or previous slide on the slides pane and the Slides tab in two ways:

- To move to the previous slide, press PAGE UP or press the up arrow.
- To move to the next slide, press PAGE DOWN or press the down arrow.

Navigate from Slide to Slide

Use the slides pane to select and move to the slide you want:

- To select a different slide, on the slides pane, scroll to the slide you want and click its thumbnail.
- To scroll to a different slide, on the slides pane, click the vertical scroll bar to move to the next or previous slide.

Move, Duplicate, or Hide Slides

As you work with the presentation you will find that the slides may work better in a different order, or being not visible at all. When creating a new slide, you may find it more efficient to copy another slide and modify it rather than to create the new one from scratch. Here is how you move, duplicate, and hide slides.

- To move a slide, on the slides pane, click the slide icon or thumbnail to be moved and drag it to the new location. An insertion point will indicate where the slide will be inserted.
- To duplicate the layout of a slide, on the slides pane, select the slide to be copied. Then, on the Home tab Slides group, click Duplicate Slide. A new slide containing the layout of the previous slide will be inserted immediately after the original one.
- To hide a slide, on the slides pane, select the slide to be hidden. Then on the Home tab Slides group, click Hide Slide. The slide will remain in the presentation but will not be displayed in the slide show. If you want to reshow it, click Hide Slide again.

Change the Look and Feel of Slides

At some point, you may want to change the look and feel of the slides in a presentation. Perhaps the slides were created for another presentation, and you want to use some of them as the basis for the next unique presentation. You may need to tweak a few components, such as the theme, color, fonts, and special effects of your slides.

Change a Theme

As you have seen, you can select a built-in (or PowerPoint standard) theme for your slides. However, you can change the themes assigned to a presentation to fit your own presentation requirements. Change the entire presentation by selecting a new theme, as you saw previously in "Find a Theme," or by altering a slide's fonts, color, and design elements.

Change Background Colors or Picture

You can change the background of a theme to be a new color, or replace the color with a picture. Figure 8-5 shows a picture used for a slide's background.

To change the background color of a slide in a presentation, follow these steps:

1. Select the slide in which you want to change the background. (If you want to change the background in all of the slides, click just one for now. You'll specify all slides later.)

Star Estates House # 345

View property
3 Bedrooms
2.5 Baths
Newly remodeled

FIGURE 8-5   You can use a picture for the background of your slides for a special effect.

2. In the Design tab Customize group, click the Format Background down arrow.

3. Choose from these options:
   - **Solid Fill**   Use a solid background color. From the pop-out menu, click the color you want.
   - **Picture From File**   Upload a picture from your computer or OneDrive to be the background of a selected slide.
   - **Apply To All**   All the slides in the presentation will have the new background color or picture.

   To undo (remove) the new background effect, press CTRL-Z.

 You cannot paste a picture copied from another presentation or from another application, such as Word or Excel. You must a select a new picture from your computer or OneDrive storage instead.

Add Animations and Transitions to Slides

Adding animation to a slide creates movement and allows you to control the timing of what the viewer sees. When you click the mouse while delivering a presentation, the animated image is moved to the screen in the position it has been dragged. You introduce objects according to what you want to discuss next.

Transitions control the overall slide movement—how one slide advances to the next. Include transitions to add interest and a sense of continuity to a presentation.

Add Animation to a Slide

To animate an object, you first select the object, then assign the animation to it, adjust it with special effects, move its timing if needed, and test it out. Follow these steps to add animation:

1. Select the object or text that you want to animate.
2. Click the Animations tab. You'll see the ribbon, shown at the top of Figure 8-6. (If the objects are unavailable—grayed out—then you have not selected an object yet.)
3. In the Animations group, click a thumbnail of the animation you want. Choose from among the following:
   - **None**   No animation. Use this to remove an animation.
   - **Appear**   The image immediately appears on the screen with no special effects.
   - **Fade In**   A dim image grows stronger from a direction you choose—top, bottom, left, or right.
   - **Fly In**   The image flies in from the direction you choose—top, bottom, left, or right.

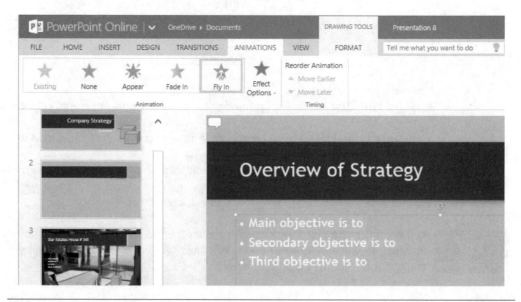

FIGURE 8-6   The Animations tab shows the ways you can animate the entry of an object.

4. Click the Effect Options down-arrow if it is available for your animation choice. If it is available, you have options about how the animation will occur, for example, the Fly In direction. Select the option you want.

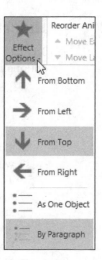

5. If you have several animations on a slide, you may want to reorder the sequence in which the animations appear. Select the object to be moved forward or backward in its display sequence. In the Animations tab Timing group, click Move Earlier or Move Later to move the selected animation before or after another.
6. To test the animation, click the Slide Show icon in the status bar. When the slide is displayed on the screen, click on the screen to advance through the animations. When you are finished, click a final time to close the slide show.

Add Transitions to a Slide

To add transitions to one or all slides, simply choose a transition from a list, choose any options about how it will be done, and select whether the transition is to apply to all slides in the presentation or just the selected slide. Figure 8-7 shows the Transitions tab.

Follow these steps:

1. Select a slide in the slides pane that will be displayed with the transition effect (that is, select the slide to which the effect will be applied, not the slide preceding it).
2. Click the Transitions tab for a list of the available transition effects.
3. Click the thumbnail of the transition effect you want:
   - **None**   No transition is applied. Use this to remove transitions.
   - **Fade**   The slide is dim and grows more vivid.
   - **Push**   The slide slides in from a direction—top, bottom, right, or left.
4. If it is available for the option you choose, click the Effect Options down arrow and select an option.
5. If you want the transition to apply to all slides in the presentation, click Apply To All.

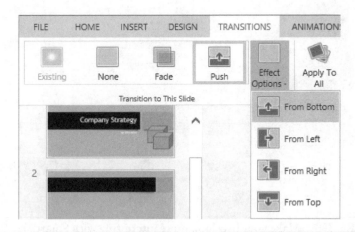

FIGURE 8-7   In the Transition tabs, select how the slides will advance on the screen.

Insert SmartArt for Lists

To make your lists artistic and professional-looking, you can choose some of the SmartArt options provided in PowerPoint. These dramatically change the look and feel of lists.

To add SmartArt, follow these steps:

1. Click Insert | SmartArt in the Illustrations group. You'll see a gallery of the possibilities for your list, as shown in Figure 8-8.
2. Click an option, and you will see the SmartArt effect on the slide. A text box with the word "Text" (to be perfectly clear) enables you to enter text into the list.
3. To change the effect, simply display the SmartArt effect gallery and select another option.
4. You can also add styles to the SmartArt. Right-click the SmartArt object in the slide, and click Style. A gallery of styles is displayed. Click the one you want.
5. When you are finished, click outside the SmartArt object.

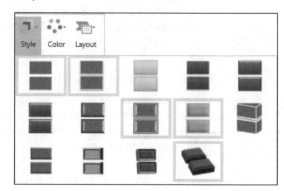

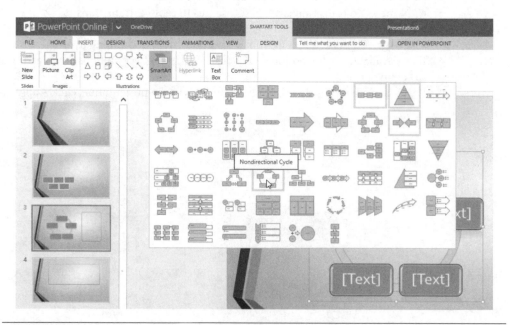

FIGURE 8-8 Make your lists look more interesting with SmartArt.

9
Working with Slide Content

This chapter covers several features that you can use to make a presentation more effective, such as notes, comments, and slide text. Preparing comments enables you to enlighten others on your team of specific points about a slide, or you can create presentation notes to help remember all you wanted to say and to help audience members follow important points.

This chapter also addresses how to work with text, from inserting a placeholder, to modifying text by editing, positioning, moving, copying, and deleting it. It also explores how to add hyperlinks to text. Finally, it explains how you can share the presentation with collaborators and control access to editing.

Work with Notes and Comments

You can create speaker notes that aid a speaker during a presentation. These notes do not appear on the slides during the slide show presentation; they are visible only for the presenter's benefit. Use comments to communicate your thoughts about a slide to your collaborators.

Create a Note

To create speaker notes, which you can print for handouts from desktop PowerPoint, use the Notes pane in Editing View (shown at the bottom of the slide in Figure 9-1). In the Notes pane, you can see a display of the slide, and below it, notes pertaining to it. Each slide has

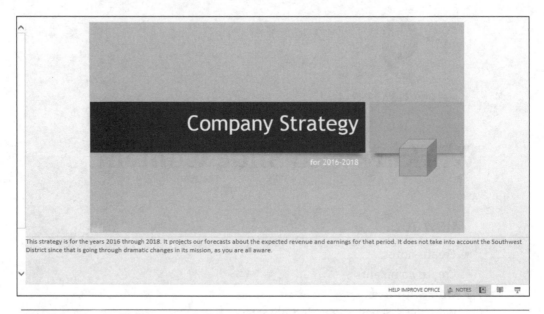

FIGURE 9-1 Below the image of the slide, in the Notes pane of the Editing View, you can add speaker notes for your presentation.

its own Notes pane for text only. You cannot add charts, graphs, or pictures to the notes. You cannot print the notes from PowerPoint Online; however, PowerPoint Online enables you to create the notes, share them with your collaborators, and then print them as handouts via desktop PowerPoint.

To create notes for your presentation, follow these steps:

1. Click in the Click To Add Notes pane at the bottom of the Presentation pane.
2. Type in notes. If you use more of the Notes pane than is available, PowerPoint will reduce the font size and line spacing so that the text will fit.

 You can also click the Notes button on the bottom right of the status bar to expand the Notes pane.

Create Comments

When you create comments, a flag is placed on the selected slide to alert viewers that comments are present. When the viewer clicks a comment, the Comments pane opens.

To create a comment, follow these steps:

1. Click Insert | Comment. A Comments pane opens on the right. A text box identifies you as the author.

2. Type your comments and press ENTER. The text box will provide a place for a collaborator's replies.

3. Click the Close icon in the upper-right corner to close the Comments pane. The Comments flags will be displayed on the slide.
4. To view a comment, click a flag. The comments will be displayed in the Comments pane.

Work with Text

Entering and manipulating text is the major part of building a presentation. Text not only includes titles and bulleted lists; it's also captions on a picture or a legend or labels on a chart. Text can be added inside a shape. Text communicates in a thousand ways. Here is how you work with text in PowerPoint.

Use a Text Layout

To create the "look" of your presentation, you will want to insert text, logos, and other pictures in a consistent way. PowerPoint provides standard layouts that enable you to do this. Earlier chapters discussed layouts when selecting a new slide. In this chapter, we are concerned with the structure of a text layout.

When you create a new blank slide, you must choose whether to use an existing layout that Microsoft provides or to create your own layout (see Figure 9-2).

Here is how to select a new layout:

1. In Editing View, click the slide immediately preceding the one you want to insert.
2. Click Home | New Slide. The New Slide dialog box is displayed, as shown in Figure 9-2.
3. Look for the placement of text, titles, and content. Examples of text placeholders are shown next. You can see a text placeholder for a title, and below it, in a smaller font, is a placeholder for text paragraph, perhaps explaining the reason for the slide. To the right is a bulleted list layout. When you type here your text will automatically be formatted in a bulleted list in the font and with the bullet depicted. Or you may decide that you prefer a picture. Beneath the bulleted list are three icons: click the leftmost icon to insert SmartArt to professionalize the content, the middle icon to insert a photo, or

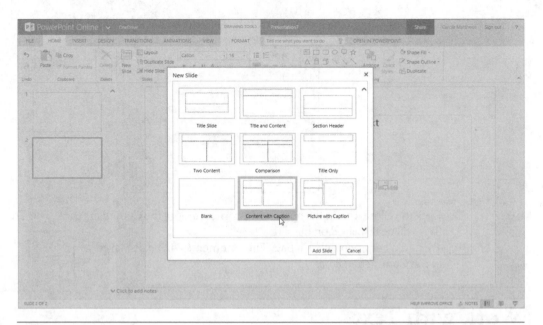

FIGURE 9-2 Choose a layout to determine how the text is structured and how it interacts with images on a slide.

the rightmost icon to insert clipart. This combination text box enables you to have a bulleted list, a photo, or clipart, but not at the same time. (You can have it all, however, by manually inserting objects using the Insert tab.)

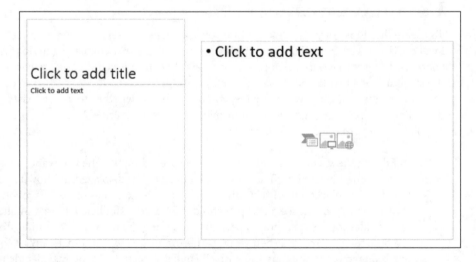

4. To enter your own text, click in the text box and type over the default text. To insert SmartArt, a photo, or clipart, click the icon and select the type of SmartArt you want, the file containing the photo, or type in the search text box the name of the type of clipart you want to find.

PowerPoint uses *text placeholders* to contain text and other objects. Text boxes can be moved, resized, or flipped. You can insert a new text box or use an existing one from a layout. The text box will be applied to the current slide. If you have not created a new slide, the layout will be applied to whichever slide is selected.

Insert a New Text Box

Even when you use a predefined layout that Microsoft provides, you will sometimes want to insert a new text box. Follow these steps:

1. Display the slide within which you will place the text box.
2. Click Insert | Text Box in the Text group. A text box is inserted into the slide.

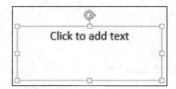

3. Place the pointer over the text box and drag it in the vicinity of where you want it placed. Don't worry too much about where the box is located; you can drag it to a precise location later. When you release the pointer, the insertion point within the text box indicates that you can begin to type text.
4. Highlight Click To Add Text and type in your text.
5. When you are finished, click outside the text box.

 When a border around a placeholder is displayed, it tells you that the text box is selected. When it is selected, there are two modes: working with text and working with the text box itself. If you click within the text box, you can enter or edit text. To then move or manipulate the text box itself, you need to click outside the text box and then move the pointer to an edge. Your pointer becomes a cross pointer, which you can drag to move the text box.

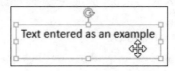

Work with Placeholders and Objects

Placeholders are containers for items, usually for text. The way you work with placeholders also works for objects, such as shapes you create. However, text boxes have some unique properties, so this section deals primarily with them.

You can work with text and text boxes by typing text into a text box, moving or copying the text box, resizing the text, positioning the text box, deleting it, filling it with color, and more.

As you type and the text reaches the edges of the text box, the words will wrap around to the next line. It may look as if the text is jumping outside the text box, but it is not. When you click outside the text box, the text will appear within.

Enter Text into a Text Box or Shape

To enter text into a text box or shape, simply click inside the item; the insertion point will appear, indicating that you can now type text. Begin to type. When you are finished, click outside the item to deselect it.

Navigate to the First or Last Character in a Placeholder

With the text in a text box selected, do the following:

- Press CTRL-HOME to move to the top left of a text box.
- Press CTRL-END to move to the last character in a text box.

Resize a Text Box or Shape

To resize a text box, you must resize the font of the text it contains. If you drag the text box handles, the usual method of resizing, you will see the text stretched to fit the text box, but when the drag is released, the text box returns to the previous size. You must change the size of the contents to change the size of the container:

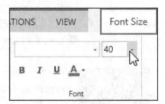

1. Click in the text box to select it and highlight the text to be resized.
2. Click Home | Font Size in the Font group and select your size choice. The text box will be resized to fit the new size of the content within it.

For a shape, simply drag the handles of the shape in the direction you want—outward to increase the size of the shape, or inward to decrease it. If you have text inside the shape, it may remain the same size. You may need to change the font size: if the text was created as a part of the graphic, it will resize with it, but if the text was created separately, it will not resize.

Delete a Text Box or Shape

To delete a text box or shape, click within a text box or shape to select it, and then press DELETE.

Copy a Text Box or Shape

To copy a text box or shape with its contents and place it in another part of the slide, follow these steps:

1. Click the text within the text box to select the text box. For a shape, simply click the shape to select it.
2. Press CTRL-C to copy the text box or shape.

3. Press CTRL-V to paste it on the slide. A duplicate will be placed on top of the first copy.

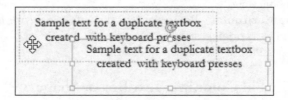

4. Drag the second text box or shape where you want it placed.

Rotate a Text Box

When you first insert a text box or shape (or click it to select it), a rotate handle appears above the text box that enables you to rotate the item in a circle. Here's how to rotate a text box:

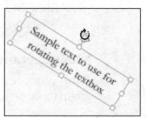

1. Place the pointer over the rotate handle. The pointer will become a darker rotate handle.
2. Drag it in the direction the text box or shape is to be rotated.
3. Click outside the text box or shape to "set" the rotation.

Position a Text Box or Shape in a Stack

Sometimes you will have overlapping objects and you'll need to move one in front of or behind another to see what you want more clearly. To move a text box, shape, or other object in a stack, follow these steps:

1. Click the item to select it.
2. Click Home | Arrange in the Drawing group to display a menu.

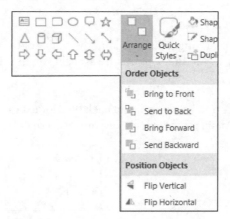

  You have these options:
  - **Bring To Front or Send To Back**   Places the selected item on the front or back of the stack.
  - **Bring Forward or Send Backward**   Places the selected item one position forward or backward in the stack.

- **Flip Vertical** Rotates or flips the item upside down. Do it twice to return it to its original state.
- **Flip Horizontal** Rotates or flips the item to a mirror image. Repeat to return the item to its original state.
3. Click outside the item to set the rotation.

Change the Fill Color in a Text Box or Shape

You may want to change the background color in a text box or shape to allow it to be seen more clearly. To change the background color of a text box or shape, you can use the Drawing Tools Format tab, Shape Styles, or the Shape Fill tool, or you can right-click to open a context menu:

1. Right-click the text box or shape, and from the context menu click Fill. A color menu is displayed.
2. Click the color you want. The text box or shape will be displayed with the new color.
3. When finished, click outside the text box or shape.

Set Paragraph Bullets and Numbering

To set your paragraph to be a bulleted or numbered list, you can use the Home tab Paragraph group tools, or you can right-click and choose the setting from the context menu:

1. Highlight the paragraph text in a placeholder or text box to be changed.
2. Click the Home tab, and in the Paragraph group, select one of the following:
   - To create a numbered list, click Numbering.
   - To create a bulleted list, click Bullets.

Align Text on a Line

You align text by centering (placing text in the center of the horizontal margins), left-justifying, or right-justifying it. All three options are available on the Home tab Paragraph group. Follow these steps:

1. Select the text to be aligned, and click the Home tab.
2. From the Paragraph group, choose one of these options:

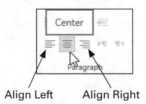

- To center text, click the Center button.
- To left-align text, click the Align Left button.
- To right-align text, click the Align Right button.

Copy Formatting with Format Painter

To copy all formatting attributes from one text box or object to another, you use Format Painter. With it, you can copy fonts, font size and style, spacing, color, alignment, and paragraph settings (such as bullets). Here's how:

1. Select the placeholder (not the text or shape within it) containing the formatting attributes to be copied.
2. Click Home | Format Painter in the Clipboard group.
3. Find the destination placeholder to contain the copied attributes, and click it.

Use Headers and Footers

You cannot insert or edit headers or footers in PowerPoint Online. However, if you have inserted them in PowerPoint desktop, you will be able to see them in your slide when they are displayed.

Move and Copy Text

You can move or copy text in at least four ways:

*   Use the cut-and-paste technique.
*   Use the Home tab on the ribbon.
*   Right-click to open a context menu and select an option.
*   Use the drag-and-drop technique.

Cut or Copy and Paste Text with the Keyboard

You can cut, copy, and paste text only in Editing View. Here's how to do it with the keyboard:

1. Select the text to be moved, and press CTRL-X to cut the text or CTRL-C to copy it.
2. Click the pointer in a text box to place the insertion point, and press CTRL-V to paste the text in the new location.

Cut or Copy and Paste with the Ribbon

The Cut command is unavailable in the ribbon in PowerPoint Online. To cut and paste text, you must copy it, paste it to the new location, and then delete the original:

1. Select the text to be moved or copied.
2. Click Home | Copy to copy it.
3. Click in a text box where you want the text inserted, and click Home | Paste in the Clipboard group.
4. To remove the original text, select it and then press DELETE.

Cut and Paste with a Context Menu

The Cut command is unavailable in the context menu. To cut and paste text, you must copy it, paste it to the new location, and then delete the original:

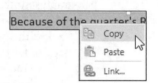

1. Select the text to be moved.
2. Right-click and click Copy.
3. Right-click the new location and click Paste.
4. To remove the original text, select it and then press DELETE.

Work with Hyperlinks

Inserting hyperlinks in a presentation enables you to link the presentation to other online files or presentations, to a web site, or to an e-mail address.

Insert a Hyperlink

To insert a hyperlink in the presentation, do the following:

1. On your slide, click where you want the hyperlink to be inserted.
2. Click Insert | Hyperlink in the Links group.
3. In the Insert Hyperlink dialog box, type the words to be inserted in the link, and then type the destination URL of the web address for the hyperlink.

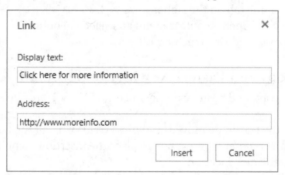

- Click in the Display Text text box and type the words that will appear in the slide. Display something obvious so the reader knows what they are to do and where they will be directed, such as "Click here for sample recipes."
- For the URL address, in your browser, load the document or web site and copy its URL. Then click in the Address text box and paste the URL. It should be in this form: http://www.someurl.com.
- If you want to place a hyperlink to an e-mail address, click in the Address text box and type the e-mail address in this form: mailto:name@someserver.com.
4. Click Insert.

Work with a Hyperlink

To edit or remove a hyperlink from text or an object, do the following:

1. Right-click the hyperlink.
2. You'll see the options, shown in the illustration, on the context menu.
3. To revise the words or URL, right-click the hyperlink and click Edit Link. The Link dialog box will be redisplayed so you can revise the Display Text or Address.
4. To copy and paste the hyperlink, right-click the hyperlink, click Copy Link, right-click where you want the link copied, and click Paste.
5. To test that the URL is correct, right-click the hyperlink and click Open Link.
6. To delete the hyperlink, right-click the hyperlink and click Remove Link.

Work with Collaborators

The advantage of PowerPoint Online is that it is easy to share with collaborators. This enables you to get others' input on the content, making the presentation more complete and accepted. Then when the presentation is ready, you can use the desktop PowerPoint version to add more sophisticated effects for final viewers, if you need to, but PowerPoint Online may be all you need. When you share a slide show, your collaborators can edit the presentation. However, you can restrict the presentation to read-only, allowing others to give you feedback but not change the slides.

You can share a presentation in three online locations: You can click the Share option on the title bar in the Editing View, or you can click File | Share. You can also find the Share option in the OneDrive display of the presentation before you request to Edit in PowerPoint Online.

Share the Presentation

You can share a presentation in two ways: you can choose to invite people so that PowerPoint creates an e-mail message with the link embedded in it, or you can have PowerPoint generate a link that you can copy and paste into an e-mail, blog, or web page that you create. When you invite someone to view your presentation, you send them an e-mail with the link to the presentation. PowerPoint provides the link to the presentation and you provide the e-mail addresses of collaborators. In the note, you may want to explain why a recipient is receiving the invitation.

When you Get A Link, PowerPoint provides the link and you copy and paste it into the e-mail or other notification method.

You can make access to the presentation read-only or a full-editing version. You also can restrict the view only to persons who have Microsoft accounts.

Share by Invitation

To enable PowerPoint to send an e-mail with the link automatically embedded, follow these steps:

1. In the Editing View, click Share on the right of the title bar. The Share banner will open, as shown in Figure 9-3. The Invite People option is the default.
2. Click in the To text box and type the e-mail address, or addresses, of your collaborator.
3. To inform your collaborator about the presentation, click in the Add A Quick Note text box and type your note.
4. Recipients Can Edit is the default. Click this and change the permission if you want to restrict the viewers to read-only or restrict the message only to those who have an Microsoft account.
5. Click Share. The Sharing message is displayed, and you'll see an indication that your collaborator has been notified and permitted access.

Get a Link

Using the Get A Link option, you get a link to the presentation from PowerPoint, copy it, and then paste it wherever you want it to be.

1. In the Editing View, click Share on the right of the title bar. The Share banner will open with the Invite People option default.
2. To have PowerPoint supply the URL of the presentation, click Get A Link. The Get A Link dialog box will be displayed.
3. Click the Choose An Option down arrow and choose whether what you are sharing can be viewed only, edited, or is public (anyone can change it).

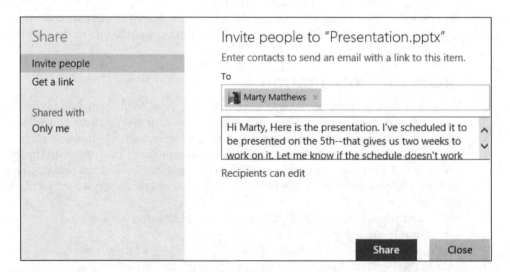

FIGURE 9-3   To share with someone, you must provide an e-mail address and determine whether the receiver can edit the presentation.

4. Click Create Link. The Edit text box will be filled with a long URL.
5. To have the link shortened, click Shorten Link. PowerPoint will automatically create a shorter, unique URL that you can use to insert into your invitation.

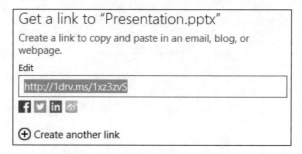

6. Highlight the link and press CTRL-C to copy it for the e-mail content
7. Click in your e-mail, web site, blog, or other medium, and press CTRL-V to paste the link.
8. Click Close to close the Share dialog box.

Remove the Link

You may want to remove the link or make it inactive. To do so, follow these steps:

1. In the Editing View, click Share on the right of the title bar. The Share banner will open with the Invite People option default.
2. Click the Shared With option.
3. Click Remove Link. The link will be removed and the dialog box closed.
4. Click Close.

10

Using OneNote Notebooks

HOW TO...

- Start OneNote and create a new notebook
- Add new sections and pages
- Add and format text
- Add and work with images
- Add and manipulate tables
- Add hyperlinks
- Find and add symbols
- Explore OneNote views
- Share, check spelling, and print pages
- Optionally edit in Desktop OneNote

In this chapter, you are introduced to Office.com's OneNote Online, the data collecting and organizing program available within Microsoft Office Online. You can think of OneNote as a virtual three-ring binder. Visualize a bookshelf containing a number of three-ring binders. You probably have the notebooks organized on the shelf by category—each notebook containing a label on its spine identifying its function. For instance, the notebooks about investing are on the left, your class notes are next to the right, your cooking notebooks are next, and so on. Within each notebook are tabs that direct you to the pages relating to that section of the notebook. The idea is the same with OneNote. Figure 10-1 displays a screenshot pointing out the similarities.

This chapter gets you started using OneNote Online. You'll review how to open it, how to create a new notebook with various sections (such as the tabs in the notebook), and how to insert new pages, each containing information about that particular section. You'll see how to access the various views available in OneNote, and how you can view authors and versions of pages. You'll see how to collaborate with others on a notebook, check your spelling, and print a page in your notebook. Finally, you'll see how to switch to OneNote desktop to make advanced editing changes, if needed (using the desktop is optional; the online version provides many features).

Notebook
section or tab

Notebook name

Page name in
the section

Page content
of the section

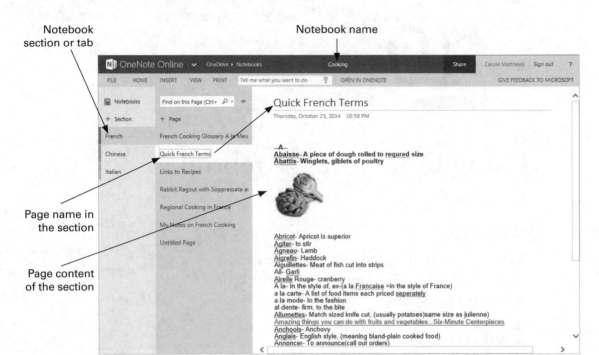

FIGURE 10-1 OneNote enables you to create a notebook with multiple sections containing multiple pages.

From here on we'll use just "OneNote" to refer to OneNote Online unless it is necessary to distinguish what is being discussed. If we need to refer to the version installed on your computer, we'll use "OneNote desktop," which will include any version of OneNote that is installed on any device and not online.

Start OneNote

Chapter 2 discussed the two ways you can start an online application, such as OneNote: using Office.com or OneDrive.com. Although they differ in how they get you to OneNote, they both are easy to use.

Start OneNote Using Office.com

To start OneNote from Office.com, follow these steps:

1. Open a browser window, type **office.com**, press ENTER, and click the OneNote Online icon to open OneNote. You may need to sign in with your Microsoft Account at this point. A Notebooks banner will be displayed, as shown in Figure 10-2.

FIGURE 10-2   From the Notebooks banner, you can create a new notebook, open an existing one, or manage your files.

2. Do one of the following:
   - Click +New to create a new blank notebook. When you're asked to name the notebook, type the name and click OK.
   - Click the icon or name of an existing notebook to open that notebook.
   - Click Manage And Delete to open the OneDrive page. From here you can open or delete files or reorganize your files and folders.

 OneNote Online will not open notebooks from Microsoft Office versions prior to 2010. In addition, file formats must have a *.one* extension to be opened.

Start OneNote Using OneDrive.com

To start OneNote from OneDrive.com, follow these steps:

1. Open a browser window, type **onedrive.com**, and sign in if asked.
2. On the OneDrive home page, do one of the following:
   - To open an existing notebook, open the folder containing the notebook and click the thumbnail of the file you want.
   - To create a new blank notebook, click Create | OneNote Notebook to open OneNote.
3. When you first create a new notebook, you'll see a text box. Type the name of your new notebook and click Create. A new blank notebook will be created and displayed.

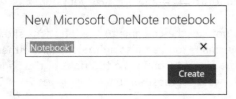

 You can upload OneNote for free onto your mobile device by accessing the store on your device (App Store in Apple devices). Search for Microsoft OneNote (don't ask Siri to do it for you on the iPhone since she looks for "one note" and doesn't find "OneNote"), and then tap the Microsoft OneNote icon to view the explanation of the program. Then tap Upload | Install to install it on your mobile.

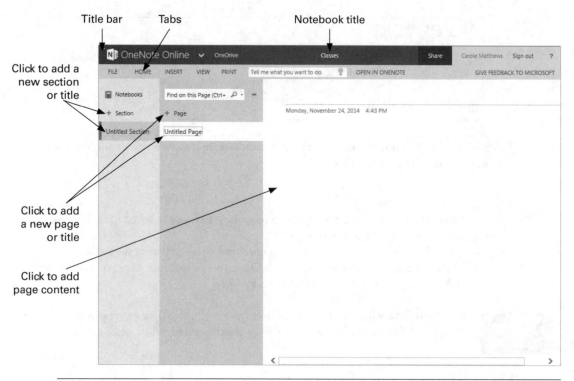

FIGURE 10-3   A blank notebook enables you to organize your content according to pages contained within sections.

Create a New Notebook

After you have created a new blank notebook, you can enter the content. The new blank notebook, shown in Figure 10-3 (if the window is large enough—see the following note), is where you begin. The notebook name is shown in the title bar. The tabs give access to the tools you'll need to add content. The blank section at the right and title pages in the middle section allow you to begin to structure and organize your notebook.

If you do not see the columns to the left, as is shown in Figure 10-3, your screen size is too small. You can display the columns either by expanding the page by clicking the Expand icon in the top right of the page, or by clicking the More icon in the left-most top position beneath the tabs.

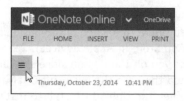

Create a New Section

A new section is like the name of a file folder, or the tab in a three-ring binder. It describes the overall content of a section of the notebook. For instance, in a Cooking notebook, the sections might be called French, Chinese, and Italian. The pages in each section contain the content, or recipes, in this case.

To create sections, follow these steps:

1. In the left column of the OneNote Online page, right-click Untitled Section and click Rename. (If you don't see the columns on the left, click the More icon on the upper left.) In the Section Name text box, type in the new name of a section in the notebook and click OK.
2. To add sections, click + Section in the left column. In the Section Name text box, type in the Section name and click OK.
3. To color-code or distinguish each section, right-click the section name and click Section Color; then click the one you want.

Any time you want to add a section, right-click any section name and select New Section. In the Section Name text box, type a name. Then you can add color or pages. (To see the section names, you may have to click the More icon first.)

Create a New Page

The pages in a section contain the content. For instance, if you are creating a cooking notebook, the pages contain the recipes and other cooking information. Initially, you will have a blank untitled page that gets its name from the title you typed in the blank page itself. (See "Enter a Page Heading" for more information.)

To create a new page:

1. At the top of the content page, click the area above the date and time line.
2. Type in a page title. This will appear as the title of the notebook page.
3. Continue to add content. See "Add Content to a Page," a bit later, for details.
4. To add pages, from the middle column, click + Page to create a new page. (To see the +Page command, you may have to click the More icon first.) You will see a new Untitled Page entry. At the top of the page in the blank heading area, type your title and add content.

To return to the view showing the columns on the left with the section and page names, you may have to click the More icon on the left.

Add Content to a Page

Adding content is, of course, the reason you create a notebook in the first place. OneNote provides a handy way to keep all information in one place, including Word documents, Excel spreadsheets, PowerPoint presentations, or links to online web sites, photos, and so on. All of these are stored in OneDrive.

Add and Format Text

Entering and manipulating text is a major part of building a notebook. Text communicates in thousands of ways. Text can include titles and bulleted or numbered lists. You can also add text inside a shape. Here is how you work with text in OneNote.

Enter a Page Title

Each section page contains a title, or heading. That title appears in the Page column of the notebook. It identifies the contents of the page. To enter a page title, follow these steps:

1. At the top of the content page, click the area above the date and time line.
2. Type a page title. The title will appear in a larger font.

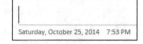

Saturday, October 25, 2014   7:53 PM

Add and Format Text

To add text, click in the text area beneath the date and time line and begin typing. You can type new text, copy and paste text from another source, or supply a link to the source. After you add text, you can format it to give it a more distinctive look.

You format text by making it bold, italics, or underline. Chapter 3 describes how to use the mini toolbar (with some unique tools) and the Font group to format text. Here's a brief review:

1. Highlight the text to be formatted.
2. In the pop-up mini toolbar, click the formatting you want. Figure 10-4 shows the mini toolbar.

 Instead of the mini toolbar, you can use the Home tab to format text. For instance, to assign a style, click Home | Styles and click the down arrow in the Styles group. The menu of options is displayed and is the same as those that appear on the mini toolbar.

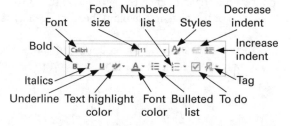

FIGURE 10-4 The mini toolbar shows many of the formatting tools.

Add Styles to Text

You also can apply a preset style, such as for a heading, which is formatted with font type, size, and color. The Styles menu contains several levels of headings, a title, citation, quote, and code.

1. Select the text to be styled. As you drag over the text, the mini toolbar is displayed.
2. Click the Styles down arrow, and from the pop-up menu choose a style.

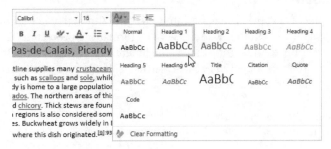

You can remove formatting from selected text by clicking Clear Formatting at the bottom of the Styles menu. You can also return the text to its regular state by clicking the Normal style.

Add a Tag

A tag is a way of assigning a category or definition to text on a page. In OneNote Online, you select a preset tag from a menu, as described below. Examples of these are the "Source for an Article" tag or "To Do."

You can add a tag to text on a page in OneNote, but you cannot search for it in OneNote Online. However, you can search for tags using OneNote desktop. So if you use tags in your notebooks using the desktop version, it may be worthwhile for you to assign them in the online version. You cannot create a unique or custom tag in OneNote Online, as you can in the desktop version, but if you have created tags and used them in notebooks using the desktop version, they will remain and be visible in the online version.

To create a tag, follow these steps:

1. Right-click in the text or paragraph to be assigned a tag.
2. In the mini toolbar, click the Tag down arrow and select your choice from the menu. You may have to scroll down to see them all.

Add a To Do Tag

You can manage a to-do list by assigning a check box tag to it and then checking it off when you're finished.

1. Right-click in the line or paragraph of your to-do list.
2. In the mini toolbar, click Tag | To Do to insert a blank check box to the left of the selected line or paragraph.

3. When the to-do task has been completed, you can indicate its status: right-click the blank check box and click Mark Tag. A red checkmark is placed in the check box, indicating that the task is complete.

4. Later, you can either remove the check box or clear the red checkmark by right-clicking the check box and choosing either Clear Tag or Remove Tag.

Add Indents to Text

You can indent text that you enter into OneNote, although you may not be able to indent text that is copied from another web site with its formatting protected. Text that is first entered can be indented only to the right—that is, the indent can be increased. Once text is indented to the right, it can then be indented to the left—that is, the indent can be decreased.

Here's how to indent text:

1. Select the line of text to be indented.
2. Right-click the selected text and click Increase Indent to move the text to the right.

To move the text back to the left, click Decrease Indent.

Highlight Text

You may want to highlight text to draw attention to it, or to remember something you want to return to. Here's how:

1. Select the text to be highlighted.
2. Right-click the selected text and click Text Highlight Color.
3. In the menu of colors, click the color you want.

To remove the highlight, right-click the color and from the mini toolbar click Text Highlight Color | No Color.

Add Color to Characters

You can color your text with the Font Color tool:

1. Select the text to which you want to add color.
2. Right-click the selected text and click Font Color.
3. In the menu of colors, click the color you want.

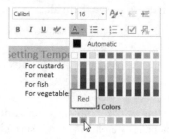

Add Bulleted or Numbered Lists

Bulleted or numbered lists help you organize data. When you create a bulleted or numbered list, the formatting will remain with every new line unless you change it—that is, every time you press ENTER, another line of the list will be created, appropriately numbered or bulleted. You can either select text after you've finished typing and format it as bulleted or numbered text, or you can format the text before you begin typing.

1. Select the text you want to make into a bulleted or numbered list. The mini toolbar is displayed.
2. Do one of the following:
   - To create a bulleted list, click Bullets on the mini toolbar. If you click the button, you'll get the default solid bullet; if you click the down arrow, you'll see options of hollow or square bullets. The bullets will be displayed to the left of the line.
   - To create a numbered list, click Numbering on the min toolbar. Again, if you click the button itself, you'll get the default numbering style; if you click the down arrow, you'll see a group of numbering options from which to choose.

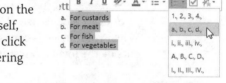

3. Click the bullet or numbering style you want. Continue typing your list.
4. When you are finished with the list and want to turn the bullets or numbering off, simply click the bullet or number button again.

Add Images to a Page

You can add pictures and clipart on a page using the Pictures group on the Insert tab.

    To add pictures or clipart, follow these steps:

1. Click below the page title in the content area of a page. (If you click in the title area, the Pictures group is unavailable.) Click where you want the image to be inserted.
2. Click the Insert tab. You have two options:
   - **Picture**   If you choose this option, Windows Explorer (or other file management program) will open, and you can navigate to and double-click the file you want. It will be uploaded to OneDrive and inserted onto the page where your pointer is located.
   - **Clip Art**   Choosing this option opens a text box, where you type a name of the type of clipart you are seeking. Then click the Search icon. From the list of possible matches, click a thumbnail to see an enlarged image on the right. Continue searching until you find an image you like. Click the thumbnail of the image and then click Insert.

3. If you want to remove an image, right-click it and click Cut.

Label or Resize Images

You cannot resize a picture by dragging on its handles. But OneNote provides an easy way for you to resize a picture. OneNote also enables you to provide alternative text for the image when the image cannot be viewed.

Resize an Image

To make an image larger or smaller, follow these steps:

1. Click the image to select it.
2. In the Picture Tools Format tab, click Format.
3. On the ribbon for the Format tab is displayed, click one of the following:
   - **Grow** Increase the size of the image.
   - **Shrink** Decrease the size of the image.
   - **Scale** Click the up or down arrow to increase or decrease the size of the image.

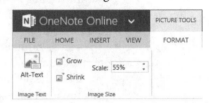

4. When your image is correctly resized, click outside the image to restore the normal tabs.

 The image cannot be dragged to another location, so you need to make sure that your pointer is located properly when you place the image.

Label an Image with Alternative Text

There are times when a viewer may not be able to see an image because of the software or device being used. In this case, you can provide alternative text so that the viewer will see a description of the image. Follow these steps to add alternative text:

1. Click the image to select it.
2. In the Picture Tools Format tab, click Format.
3. In the ribbon for the Format tab, click Alt-Text.
4. In the Alternative Text dialog box, type the text that will be displayed instead of the image, when needed.
5. Click OK.

 A useful OneNote Help site compares the OneNote desktop version with the OneNote Online version. In Online OneNote, click the Help icon (question mark) in the upper-right corner, type **differences** in the search box, and then click the Search icon (magnifying glass). If you are an experienced user of OneNote, you'll appreciate learning about the differences between the two products.

Add Tables

You can use tables for tabular data or to organize content into rows and columns, as shown in Figure 10-5. In this table, we define the content of the French cooking section with a simple table of links rather than individual pages of recipes.

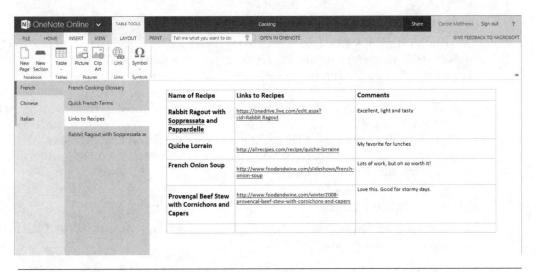

FIGURE 10-5   Tables are useful for to organize your content.

Here's how to add a table:

1. On the page, click in the content area where you want the table inserted.
2. Click Insert | Table.
3. In the diagram of rows and columns, drag over the number of rows and columns you want on your page, as shown here. The table in Figure 10-5 shows three columns and six rows, for example.

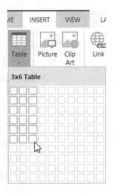

Manipulate Tables

To work with tables, you can access a special contextual tab that is available only when a table, or an element within the table, such as a row, column, or cell, is selected. Figure 10-6 shows the Layout tab's tools. The tools are grouped and named by function.

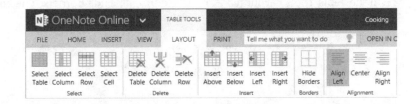

FIGURE 10-6   The Table Tools Layout tab contains tools for working with tables.

Select Table Elements

To select an element within a table, such as the table itself, or a row, column, or cell, you first click the table or element and then select the appropriate icon from the Select group in the Layout tab. This tab is displayed only when the table is selected.

1. To select the table itself (or an individual row, column, or cell) click in the table (or row, column, or cell).
2. In the Table Tools Layout tab Select group, click the element you want to select. It will be highlighted on the page. At this point, you can delete or insert information (see the appropriate sections a bit later).

Delete a Table Element

To remove a table element, such as the table, row, or column, you use the Table Tools Layout tab to select the element and then delete it:

1. To delete the table itself (or an individual row or column), click in the table (or row or column).
2. In the Table Tools Layout tab Select group, click the element to select it.
3. In the Delete group, click the element you want to delete. It will be removed.

Insert a Column or Row

When you insert a row, you can insert it above or below the row where your pointer is located. Likewise, when you insert a column, it can be to the right or the left of the column you clicked.

1. To insert a row or column, click in a cell in the row or column next to the one you will insert.
2. In the Table Tools Layout tab Insert group, click the tool to insert the row or column above, below, to the left, or to the right of the row or column you clicked. A new row or column will be inserted.

Hide Table Borders

You can hide the table borders that separate the rows and columns of a table. Follow these steps:

1. To hide the borders of a table, click somewhere in the table.
2. In the Table Tools Layout tab Borders group, click Hide Borders. The borders on the table will be hidden.

Name of Recipe	Links to Recipes	Comments
Rabbit Ragout with Soppressata and Pappardelle	https://onedrive.live.com/edit.aspx?cid=Rabbit Ragout	Excellent, light and tasty
Quiche Lorrain	http://allrecipes.com/recipe/quiche-lorraine	My favorite for lunches

3. To make the borders show again, click Hide Borders again.

Align Content in a Table

You can left-align, center, or right-align content in a table. Normally, you would do this for a column you want to be aligned differently than the default left-align. The important step is to select the table row or column or cell that is to be aligned first. You can even change the alignment of the entire table. It's important to select correctly; otherwise, you may align the contents of only one cell, rather than the row or column you expected.

Follow these steps to align text:

1. Click in the cell, row, or column to be aligned.
2. In the Table Tools Layout tab Select group, click the element to be aligned.
3. In the Layout tab Alignment group, click the alignment you want for the selected element.

Add Web Links

You can also add web links to web pages. The table in Figure 10-5 shows how links can be used instead of including the actual recipe content. The links can be to pages within your notebook, other notebook pages, or unconnected web pages. For example, in the middle section of Figure 10-5 you'll see that a page for rabbit ragout is listed, showing the actual destination for the link on the displayed page. However, the other links are to non-notebook destinations.

To insert links to documents, spreadsheets, or presentations stored on OneDrive or elsewhere, follow these steps:

1. Click in the page where you want the link inserted.
2. Click Insert | Link in the Links group.
3. In the Link dialog box, type the Display Text words that will appear on the page.

4. Type the Address URL of the link.
5. Click Insert.

The address and the display text can be the same, but often you'll want a short display phrase that tells what the link is without actually showing the longer URL.

 If you want to change the display text or address of the link, right-click the link and select Edit Link. You'll see the dialog box where you can edit the contents.

Manipulate a Link

You can change a link, test it, copy it, or delete it.

1. Right-click the link to be manipulated.
2. In the pop-up menu, choose one of the following:
   - **Edit Link** Change the display text or address.
   - **Select Link** Select the link so you can do something with it, such as copy it.
   - **Open Link** Test the link to see if it works correctly.
   - **Copy Link** Copy the link so you can paste it somewhere else using the Paste command.
   - **Remove Link** Delete the link.

Add a Symbol

You can add a symbol, such as a copyright or trademark symbol, that is not on the keyboard. Follow these steps:

1. Click in the page where you want the symbol inserted.
2. Click Insert | Symbol in the Symbol group.
3. Click the symbol you want from the menu.

 If you want to use a symbol that is not on the list, you can request that Microsoft insert it. Click Insert | Symbol and then click Request A New Symbol. You will be asked to submit a form requesting that the symbol be added. Although there's no promise that the symbol will be added, Microsoft does pay attention to feedback like this.

Explore OneNote Views

OneNote has two notebook views: Editing View and Reading View. You can also show the authors of a notebook or show the various versions of it.

Use Editing View

You'll most often be using Editing View. It is designed to allow you to change and add content easily to a notebook. When you open a notebook by clicking it, this is the default view. Here is how you find it:

- In Reading View, click Edit Notebook | Edit In OneNote Online.
- In OneDrive, find the notebook you want and click it.
- If authors or page versions are shown, click View | Editing View.

Use Reading View

In Reading View, you see your notebook without the editing tabs and commands. It is less obstructed and "cleaner" looking. If you are a collaborator on a notebook, this view can be quickly used to see what is contained in the notebook; then you can switch to Editing View to make quick changes. If you are in Editing View, click View | Reading View.

Show Authors and Page Versions

One of the benefits of using Office is its collaboration ability. The Show Authors and Versions views are part of this feature. When you share a notebook with others, you can specify that they can edit it as well. When others make changes, you immediately see the changes on your computer. Tracking who has made the changes, and which changes they have made, is what the Show Authors and Versions commands are for. Here's how:

1. In Editing View, click the View tab.
2. Choose from the following options in the Authors and Versions groups:
    *   **Show Authors**   See who has made changes to a page. On the far right of a page, you'll see the names. Click Show Authors again to return to the Editing View.
    *   **Versions**   View revisions and who has made them. The versions will be displayed beneath the page title in the Page column. Figure 10-7 shows this. If you click a specific version, it will be displayed in the page content area with a message identifying the version.

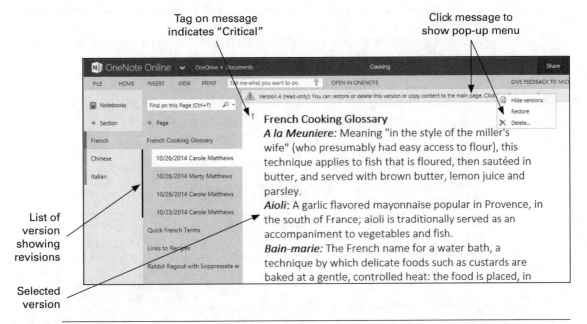

FIGURE 10-7   Showing versions of a notebook enables you to track changes and who made them.

Perform Other Functions with OneNote

You can perform several other common functions with OneNote. As with the other online apps, you can easily use OneNote to share a notebook with collaborators, so that you can get other opinions on the content, making it more complete and accepted. When you share a notebook, your collaborators can edit the content. However, you can restrict the access to read-only, allowing others to give you feedback but not change it. You also can perform spell-checks on the OneNote content and print pages. In addition, if you want to use the features available only with OneNote desktop, it's easy to do.

Share the Notebook

You can share a notebook in three ways: You can use the Share option on the title bar in Editing View, click File | Share, or click the Share option in Reading View. If you choose the Invite People option, OneNote creates an e-mail message with the link to the notebook embedded in it; or you can choose Get A Link, and OneNote generates a link that you can copy and paste into an e-mail, blog, or web page that you create. OneNote provides the link to the notebook and you provide the e-mail addresses of collaborators. In the note, you can explain why a recipient is receiving the invitation.

You can make the access to the notebook to be read-only or a full-editing version. You also can restrict the document only to persons who have Microsoft accounts.

Share by Invitation

To allow OneNote to send an e-mail with the link automatically embedded, follow these steps:

1. In Editing View, click Share at the right of the title bar. The Share banner will open, as shown in Figure 10-8. The Invite People option is the default.

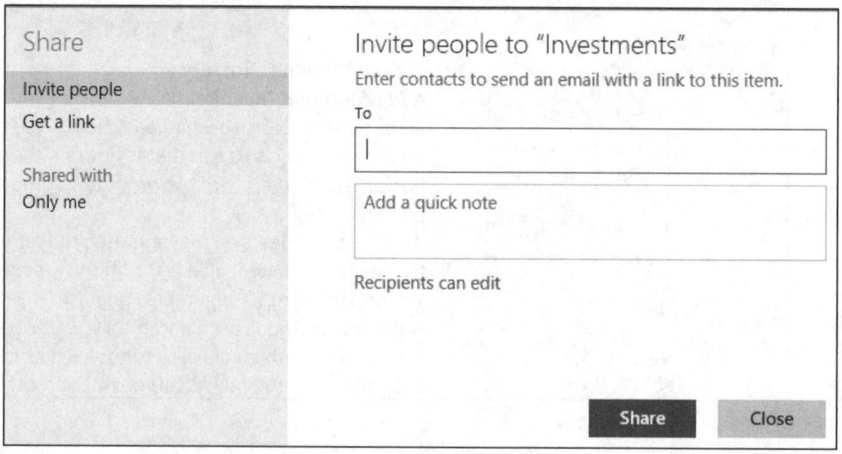

FIGURE 10-8   To share with someone, you must provide an e-mail address and indicate whether they can edit the notebook.

2. Click in the To text box and type the e-mail address or addresses of the collaborator(s).
3. To inform the collaborator(s) about the notebook, click in the Add A Quick Note text box and type a note.
4. Click Recipients Can Edit and change the permission if you want to restrict the viewers to read-only or if you want to send the e-mail only to those who have a Microsoft account.
5. Click Share. The Sharing message will be displayed, and you'll see an indication that your collaborator(s) has been notified and the permitted access.

Get a Link

Click the Get A Link option to get a link to the notebook from OneNote; then you can copy and paste it wherever you want.

1. In Editing View, click Share at the right of the title bar. The Share banner will open with the Invite People option default.
2. To have OneNote supply the URL of the notebook, click Get A Link.
3. In the Get A Link dialog box, click the Choose An Option down arrow and choose whether the notebook can be viewed only, edited, or is public (anyone can view it).
4. Click Create Link.
5. The Edit text box will contain a long URL address. To shorten the URL, click Shorten Link.

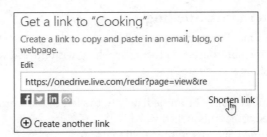

6. Highlight the link and press CTRL-C to copy it.
7. Click in your e-mail, web site, blog, or other medium, and press CTRL-V to paste the link.
8. Click Close to close the Share dialog box.

Remove the Link

You can remove the link or make it inactive:

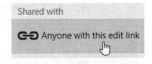

1. In Editing View, click Share at the right of the title bar. The Share banner will open with the Invite People option default.
2. Click the Anyone With This Edit Link option.
3. The Remove Link button appears next to the Close button. Click Remove Link. The link will be removed and the dialog box will be closed.
4. Click Close.

Change Permission to Share

You can change a person's access to a notebook, to give them less or more editing ability:

1. In Editing View, click Share at the right of the title bar. The Share banner will open with the Invite People option default.
2. At the lower left, click the permission you want to change. The person's name and e-mail will be displayed to the right.
3. Click the down arrow beneath the e-mail address and choose the option you want.

Check Spelling

You have limited, but important, spell-check capability in OneNote. OneNote will automatically check your spelling, and if it finds a word that it cannot match to the dictionary, it underlines it with a red wavy line. You have some options. If it is a normal word that the spelling checker may know, it gives you a list of alternatives. You can choose one of the suggested alternatives or ignore the suggestions. Perhaps the word just isn't in the dictionary, or perhaps you know the word is correct as spelled, such as a person's name. You can also check a word for correct spelling in another language.

Find an Alternative Spelling

As mentioned, OneNote automatically flags all words in a page that it cannot find in its dictionary. If OneNote alerts you to a misspelling with the red wavy line, and you want to seek an alternative, follow these steps:

1. Place your cursor in or immediately to the left of the word so that the spelling checker finds the correct misspelled word.
2. Click Home | Spelling in the Spelling group.

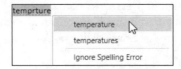

3. In the menu displayed, do one of the following:
   - If the correct word is suggested, click it and it will replace the misspelled word.
   - If you want to remove the red wavy line, click Ignore Spelling Error.

 A quicker way to invoke the spelling checker is to right-click the misspelled word and click the suggested word from the list.

Check Spelling for a Different Language

If you are working with words from a foreign language and you're not sure of the spelling, OneNote enables you to check a word quickly using a foreign language dictionary. Or perhaps you

FIGURE 10-9   Select a specific language to check the spelling of a foreign word.

know the word is spelled correctly, but you want to remove the red wavy line. If a flagged word is correctly spelled in the specified language, the spelling checker will remove the red wavy line.

1. Right-click the word.
2. From the pop-up menu with alternatives, select Set Proofing Language.
3. In the Language dialog box, shown in Figure 10-9, find the correct language option and click it.
4. If you do not want the spelling checked, click the Don't Check Spelling check box to place a checkmark within it. You might choose this if you want the red wavy line removed.
5. Click OK. If the word is correctly spelled (or not checked), the red wavy line will be removed. Otherwise, you can get suggestions in the usual way.

Edit the Notebook in Desktop OneNote

If you find that OneNote is excellent for sharing with others, but lacks the full editing features of Desktop OneNote, you can easily transfer your online notebook to the desktop version of OneNote software. Here's how:

1. In Editing View of OneNote Online, click the Open In OneNote tab.
2. If your browser asks whether you want to allow the web site to access your computer, click Allow.
3. OneNote desktop will show your notebook open. The OneNote online version will remain open as well.
4. Any editing changes you make to the desktop version will be synchronized to the online version.

Note   You can also get to OneNote desktop by clicking File | Info | Open In OneNote.

Print with OneNote

You can print a notebook or a portion thereof in OneNote Online, or you can "print" a page in a notebook to a computer location, so that you can insert it into another notebook. This is one way to build a notebook section made up of several pages from other notebooks.

Follow these steps:

1. From Editing View, click the Print tab.
2. In the Print dialog box, shown in Figure 10-10, choose from among the following:
   - Select the printer that you want, either a normal printer or an Office 2010 or 2013 OneNote file to copy to another file.
   - If you don't see the printer you want, such as a regular printer, click Find Printer and find the computer or network with the printer you want to use. Then double-click the printer name.
   - To change the print orientation from Portrait to Landscape, click Preferences | Orientation, and then choose Landscape. Then click OK.
   - To print specific pages only, select Pages, and in the text box, type the range of pages you want, such as "1–3".
   - To print more than one copy, change the Number Of Copies.

FIGURE 10-10 You can print or copy portions of a notebook to a printer or another computer file in the Print dialog box.

3. Click Print.
4. If you have chosen a regular printer, the page will be printed. If you have chosen another OneNote "printer," Desktop OneNote will display a OneNote screen with the Select Location in OneNote dialog box open. Find the notebook section you want the current pages inserted into, click it, and then click OK. The online page will be inserted into the section. At this point, if you select the page to be printed, and then click File | Print | Print Preview, you can see what will be printed. When it is correct, click Print.

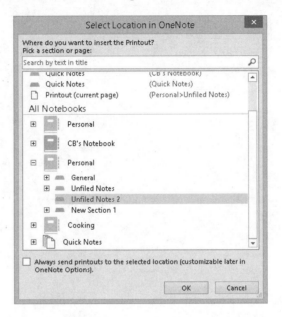

If you are printing to another location (step 4), you may have to start OneNote for the first time. In this case, OneNote will want to sync automatically with OneNote Online. If you allow this, you will never see the dialog box in step 4. If you do not sync, however, you'll be able to complete the step.

11

Using and Managing Outlook, Calendar, and People

HOW TO...

- Create and send e-mail
- Arrange, sort, and select e-mail
- Open and display the calendar
- Create a new appointment, event, task, or birthday
- Add and filter calendars
- Manage your people
- Work with groups

In this chapter, you are introduced to Office.com's Outlook, Calendar, and People, the contact file. Outlook.com has integrated these three applications so that they seamlessly work together to manage your e-mail communications, time, and contacts, although they are treated as separate applications rather than being combined as they are within Office Outlook on the desktop. These applications enable you to send and receive e-mail, keep track of events in your calendar, and manage your contacts.

Work with Outlook

To set up an Outlook.com e-mail account, you must have a Microsoft account. If you have a Microsoft account, you'll just need to enter your e-mail address and password. If you don't have a Microsoft account, you'll have to set one up, connecting it with any e-mail addresses. Then you can begin to work with Outlook.com. Chapter 1 shows you how to get to and use the sign-up page.

For a quick review of creating a Microsoft account, enter **microsoft sign up page** in your browser search box and click the search icon or button. In the search results, find an entry that enables you to sign up for Microsoft, and click it. If necessary, keep following the prompts to create a new Microsoft account until you see a form that needs to be filled in. You'll need an e-mail address, password, and phone number in addition to your name and address. Complete the form and click Create Account to finish. Be sure to remember your password.

Get Started with Outlook.com

Once an overall Microsoft account is established, you'll be able to set up the Outlook.com account. A common way to open Outlook.com is from Office.com. Once you've set up your Outlook.com account, you can create new e-mails, reply to e-mails, delete e-mails, arrange your e-mail into folders, and more. But first you need to associate Outlook Online with an e-mail address and get your contacts uploaded.

 You can also get to Outlook.com by typing **Outlook.com** as the browser URL. Or, from Calendar or Contact, you can click the down arrow next to the logo name and select Outlook.com (as of the writing of this book the logo down-arrow is not implemented).

To associate Outlook Online with an e-mail address and get your contacts uploaded, follow these steps:

1. Type **office.com** into your browser URL text box.
2. On the Office Online page, click Outlook.com. You'll be asked if you want to create an alias e-mail address, as shown in Figure 11-1. You can create a new Outlook.com e-mail address, an alias such as *somename@outlook.com*, to receive and send e-mail with a different e-mail, but possibly using the same password as your normal e-mail address. Click Create An Alias if you want to do this. You'll first need to enter your Microsoft account password, and then enter a new alias or e-mail address. You can create multiple aliases.

FIGURE 11-1 The Outlook.com welcome page enables you to create an alias.

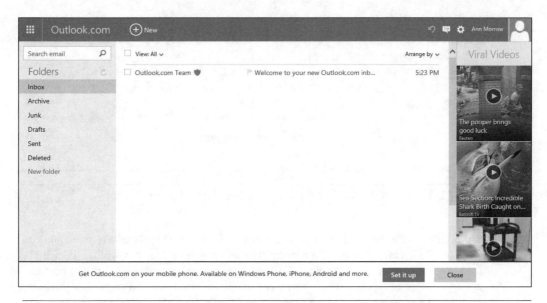

FIGURE 11-2   Create and send e-mail in the Outlook.com home page.

3. If you do not want to create an alias at this time, click Skip For Now. You'll have another opportunity to do this.

4. You'll next see the main Outlook.com page, as shown in Figure 11-2. Click the first e-mail you have, "Welcome to the Outlook.com inbox." This opens your first e-mail, which gives you some tips on how to get started. The menu bar contains the tools you need to create and send e-mail, delete or archive e-mail, define or move e-mail to unique folders, or categorize e-mail by type.

Create a New E-mail

You can easily create new e-mail in Outlook.com:

1. Click New (with a circle + icon) in the title bar. The e-mail shown in Figure 11-3 shows an e-mail message ready to send.

2. In the To text box, begin to type the name or e-mail address of the person you are contacting. As you type the name, matching contacts will be displayed. If you see the correct one, click it. If the person is not in your contact list, type the e-mail address. (You can enter the contact's name in the People app.)

3. To send a copy of the e-mail to someone else, click Cc and type a contact name or e-mail address.

4. To send a blind copy to someone (where the primary or Cc recipients will not see the Bcc recipient), click Bcc and type a contact name or e-mail address.

5. Click in the Add A Subject area and type the subject of the e-mail.

FIGURE 11-3 Write an e-mail message using Outlook.com.

6. Click in the Add A Message area and type your message. You have these options:
   - **To format text or add a hyperlink or emoticon**, use the toolbar. Figure 11-4 shows the options in the toolbar. To format text, select it and then click the button. To insert something, click where you want the object inserted, and then click the button.
   - **To attach a file, inline picture, or OneDrive link**, click Insert in the menu bar and select your choice.
   - **To save your e-mail** to return to it later, click Save Draft in the menu bar. It will be saved in the Drafts folder.
   - **To convert to Rich Text, Plain Text, or to Edit in HTML**, click Options in the menu bar and select your choice.
   - **To delete the e-mail**, click Cancel | Delete.
7. When you're finished, click Send in the menu bar to send the e-mail.

Arrange E-mail into Folders

You can create new folders and establish rules for managing the inflow of e-mail. For instance, if you always want to delete e-mail from Joe, you can create a rule to do so. If you always want to place an incoming e-mail from Joy into a Friends folder, you can create a new folder and a rule to do so.

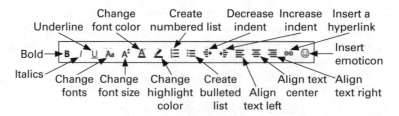

FIGURE 11-4 The e-mail message toolbar offers formatting options.

Create New Folders

You can create new folders and arrange them according to your needs. For instance, you can create a Friends folder or a Projects folder for e-mail from friends or relating to projects you are working on. You might want to do this to be able to track all e-mail from particular people or e-mail about a particular subject. You might place the folders inside another folder so that you can easily find them. Follow these steps to create new folders:

1. Under Folders, click New Folder.
2. In the blank text box, type the name of the new folder.
3. Drag the folder where you want it in the list of folders, perhaps under Inbox or some other descriptive folder. An arrow to the left of the receiving folder will indicate that there are folders under it. The arrow faces to the right when the folder is closed and down when it is open. You can see the added folders when the arrow indicates the receiving folder is open.

Create Rules

When you receive e-mail, it is automatically placed in your Inbox. You can drag e-mail messages into another folder after you've read them, or you can create rules so that Outlook.com automatically places them in another folder. Here's how:

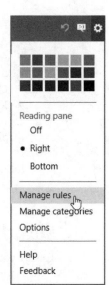

1. Click the gear icon in the title bar, and choose Manage Rules. The first time you will have no rules, so click New to start one.
2. On the Rules For Sorting New Messages, click New. The Create Rule banner will display, an example of which is shown in Figure 11-5. In this case, e-mail received from someone@isp.com will be automatically placed into a folder named Project A.
3. Click the When An Email Matches down arrow and select an option:
   - **Sender Contains** when you want to select e-mails based on the sender's e-mail address.
   - **Recipient Contains** when you want to select e-mails based on the recipient's e-mail address.
   - **Older Than** when you want to select e-mail before a given number of days. You may want to place older mail in a "non-active" folder, for instance.

FIGURE 11-5 You can create a rule to delete or sort e-mail depending on certain criteria.

- **Not the Latest** when you want to select e-mail that is not the most recent you have received. Then choose if it is not the most recent 1, 3, 5, or 10 you have received.
- **Subject Contains** when you want to select e-mail based on the subject of the e-mail, which you stipulate.
- **Keyword Contains** when the e-mail contains certain words that you provide.
- **Category Is** when the e-mail has been assigned to a certain category that you select.
- **Category Is Not** when the e-mail has been assigned to any category except the selected one.
- **Attachment** when an e-mail either has an attachment or doesn't have one. You select which.

4. Click the Do The Following down arrow and select the action to be taken:
   - **Delete** to place the e-mail in the Delete folder.
   - **Move To** to move the e-mail to a named folder, which you select. It may be Inbox or a folder you have created.
   - **Mark As Junk** to move the e-mail to the Junk folder
   - **Archive** to move the e-mail to the Archive folder.
   - **Mark As** to mark the e-mail automatically as being read or unread.
   - **Set Flag State** to flag or unflag the e-mail.
   - **Categorize As** to assign a category to the e-mail, which you select.
   - **Remove Category** to remove a given category from an e-mail.

5. If you want to create an additional condition or action, click +Condition or +Action to display another potential rule. Repeat steps 3 and 4.
6. If you want to delete a condition or action after you have created it, click the trash icon following the condition or action.
7. When you are finished, click Create Rule.

Sort the Display of E-mail

To sort your e-mail for a quick search for specific e-mail, or to see the extent of certain conversation threads more clearly, follow these steps:

1. To sort your e-mail messages, click the Arrange By down arrow above the displayed e-mail.

2. You have these options:
   - **Date** to sort by the date received.
   - **From** to sort by the sender's name.
   - **Subject** to sort by the e-mail's subject.
   - **Size** to sort by the e-mail's size.
   - **Conversation** to sort the e-mail into conversation threads.
3. After you have sorted e-mail for a specific purpose, you can re-sort it quickly into its normal sequence by choosing to arrange by date.

Display Selected E-mail

You can display only certain e-mails. Follow these steps:

1. To display specific e-mail messages, click the View down arrow above the displayed e-mail.
2. You have these options:
   - **All** to view all e-mail messages.
   - **Unread** to see quickly what you've missed reading.
   - **Contacts** to sort by contacts.
   - **Groups** to see what group discussions you have received.
   - **Newsletters** to view newsletter e-mails that you receive.
   - **Social Updates** to view updates from Google, Facebook, or other social networks.
   - **Everything Else** to view everything else not included in this list.
3. After you have displayed an isolated list, you can quickly return to the previous view by selecting View All.

Manage Your Calendar

Your primary calendar lists all appointments, events, birthdays, and U.S. holidays that it knows about. Many of these are entered into the calendar automatically, coming from your People list, which imports birthdays from your mobile devices, tablets, and social networks. You add your own calendar entries to track specific events and tasks. You can filter types of calendar entries so that not so many appear on the calendar or that only the ones you want appear, such as a list of tasks. In addition to the main calendar that contains all entries, a personal calendar is created automatically.

Open and Display the Calendar

The primary calendar is what you see when you open the Calendar app. Here is how you access it and control the display of events:

1. Open Office.com and click Calendar. The Welcome To Calendar banner is displayed.
2. Sign on with your Microsoft account if requested, set your time zone, and click Continue To Calendar.

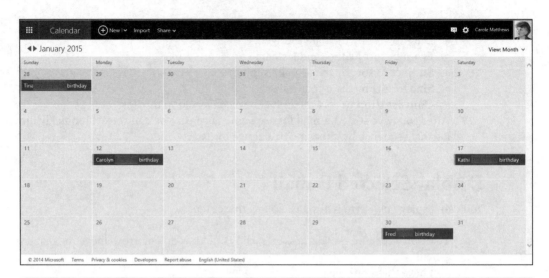

FIGURE 11-6 The Calendar imports dates it knows about from other social networks and contact lists.

3. You will see your calendar filled with what it knows about from your social networks and mobile phone connections (see Figure 11-6). You have the following options:

   - To alter the month being displayed, click the arrows to the left of the month displayed at the top of the calendar. Click the left arrow to go to the previous month, and click the right arrow to go forward one month.
   - To change the time period displayed by the calendar, click the View down arrow on the far right of the displayed date. Choose between displaying your events by Month, Week, Day, Agenda (a list of events scheduled for the day), or Task (add or change a task's status). You designate a new appointment as being an event or task when you create it.
   - To hide entries on a calendar so that only the ones you want are showing, click the gear icon on the menu bar. From the drop-down menu, remove the checkmark from any calendars you want to hide. Place a checkmark next to those you want to see.

You can always return to the calendar default view by clicking Calendar in the upper-left corner of the page. If the view is not what you expect, check the View to make sure you have not reset the default. You can always switch to another online application (for example, back and forth between Outlook.com, People, and Calendar) by clicking the square icon to the left of the Calendar title.

Create a New Appointment

You can quickly add an appointment to your calendar, such as personal reminders or pertinent appointments. To create a new entry in a Calendar, follow these steps:

1. Click in a calendar day and a dialog box will open.

2. Click in the Subject text box and type a name for your appointment or reminder.
3. Set the Start time and How Long the appointment is expected to last.
4. Click Save.
5. If you want to enter additional details, such as the location, click View Details and then Save. To find out more about details, read the next section, "Add an Event, Task, or Birthday."

Add an Event, Task, or Birthday

In some cases you'll want to add more information, perhaps the names of those whom you're meeting, the details of a task, or the location of a meeting, or you may want to add a charm so you can tell at a glance the purpose of the event. Also, by creating an event, task, or birthday, you can separate the events in your calendar views. The information you have available will differ depending on the type of entry you create. Here's how to add an event, task, or birthday:

1. In the Calendar view, click the New down arrow. You'll see a menu with these options:
   - **Event**   Schedule an appointment.
   - **Task**   Define a task or project.
   - **Birthday**   Set up a reminder for someone's birthday.
   - **Calendar**   Create a calendar for organizing appointments. (see "Add Another Calendar," later in this chapter).

2. Select an option and continue using the corresponding steps described in the following sections.

Add an Event or Appointment

An event is an appointment of some kind. It has a time and date, a location, and it may be a repeating event. It can be business or personal. You may decide to display it in a selected calendar, and you may want to invite others in a collaborative project to view it.

1. Click New | Event to schedule an appointment. In the form shown in Figure 11-7, you have the following options:
   - On the top of the right column, click Add A Subject, if it hasn't been automatically selected, and type the name of the event or appointment. Below the name, click Add A Description and type a brief summary of the entry.
   - Click the When and Start down arrows and select an option.
   - Click How Long down arrow to choose how long you expect the meeting to last.
   - Click in the Location text box and type where the meeting is being held.
   - Click the Calendar down arrow to choose in which calendar you want the appointment to appear.
   - Click the How Often down arrow to indicate how often you expect this appointment time to be repeated.
   - Click Charm to insert an icon in the appointment so that you can see at a glance what kind of an appointment it is.

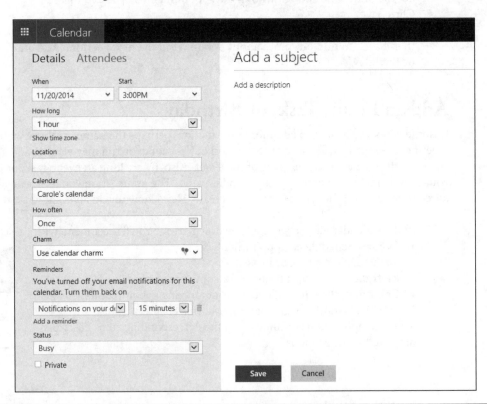

FIGURE 11-7 The form for adding an event or appointment enables you to capture important information about it.

- Click the Reminders down arrow to choose how you want notification to be sent and how often. If you really don't want to forget this appointment, click Add A Reminder to add one or more reminders.
- Click the Status down arrow to set your availability for the time slot you have. Is this time reserved? Pending? Free? Are you away at this time?
- Finally, click the Private check box if you don't want to share this appointment with others.

2. Click Attendees at the top of the left column and enter or select people to invite to your event.
3. Click Save to save the event and display it on the designated calendar.

Add a Task

A task can be a one-time task or an overall project broken into smaller tasks. It can be a to-do list of sorts. A task is not displayed in the calendar; instead, it is displayed as a list when you filter the calendar by selecting Task. To add a task, follow these steps:

1. Click New | Task to describe a task or project entry. You have these options:
   - In the right column, where the insert pointer is, type the name of the task or project. Below the name, click Add A Description and type a brief summary of the entry.
   - In the left column, click Calendar to choose another calendar for this task.
   - Click Due Date and Time to set your deadline.
   - Click Status to set the status of the task.
   - Click Priority to set how important this task is.
   - Click Reminders to establish how you will be notified of the pending date and how often.
2. Click Save to save the task and display it on the designated calendar.

  To view your task list, click View | Task on the far right of the screen. You'll see a list of your pending tasks. To see completed tasks, click Completed. If you want to change the task from Completed to In Progress, remove the checkmark from the check box. The color tab on the left shows which calendar holds the Task entry.

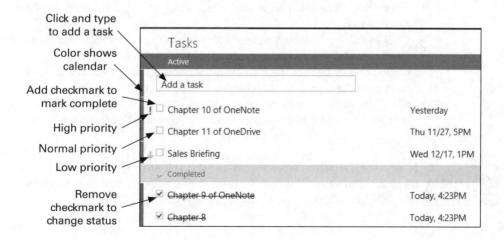

Click and type to add a task

Color shows calendar

Add checkmark to mark complete

High priority

Normal priority

Low priority

Remove checkmark to change status

Remember a Birthday

One of the most useful events you can have on a calendar is a reminder of someone's birthday. If the birthday person is in your People list already, the birthday will be added to the person's information. If the person is not in People, he or she will be added when you add their birthday to the calendar.

1. Click New | Birthday to enter a birthday on the calendar. You have these options:

   - Under Details, click in the First Name and Last Name text boxes to enter the name of the person.
   - Click the Birthday down arrows and select the month, day, and year of the birthday.
   - Click Charm to insert an icon in the birthday listing, for instance, the birthday cake.
   - Click Add A Reminder to add one or more reminders to be sent to you.
2. Click Save to save the birthday.

Add Another Calendar

You can create multiple calendars for different purposes. Perhaps you want a personal calendar and another calendar for business. Perhaps you belong to a club or organization and want to track those appointments separately. The calendars can be distinguished by color that show on the calendar so they can be easily identified. Here is how to add a calendar:

1. Click New | Calendar. A form is displayed with these options:
   - Click in the Calendar Name text box and type the name.
   - Place a checkmark in the Calendar Color you want to be assigned to the entries for that calendar.
   - Click the Charm down arrow and select an icon to be assigned to all the entries in this calendar.
   - Click in the Description text box and type a summary of what the calendar contains.
   - Click Edit Sharing to be able to share the calendar with others.
   - Click either or both of the E-mail Notifications check boxes to select whether you want reminders for events and tasks, and/or whether you want a daily agenda.
   - Click the Notifications down arrow to set how you want to receive calendar notifications and how often. Click Add A Reminder to add more.
2. Click Save to finalize the new calendar.

To edit the definition information about a calendar, click the gear icon on the menu bar and select Options. In the Options page, click the name of the calendar you want to edit. You can also add a calendar from this page.

Filter Calendar Entries

Your calendar can become so crowded with entries that it is hard to see the important ones. You can filter the types of entries you see. To filter an entry type (such as from the birthday calendar or the U.S. Holidays), causing it to be hidden, you remove the checkmark next to the entry.

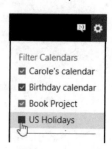

1. Click the gear icon on the menu bar, and a menu is displayed with selected entries.
2. Under Filter Calendars, verify that the checkmarks are next to the entries you want to see.
3. Remove the checkmarks next to any options you want to hide.

Import Calendar Entries

You can import calendar entries into an existing calendar or a new one by following these steps:

1. Click Import on the menu bar.
2. In the Import page, choose whether you want to import into an existing calendar or into a new one.
3. Browse to where the calendar you want to import is located and select it.
4. If you are importing into a new calendar, click in the Calendar Name and enter the name to be assigned to the new calendar.
5. If you are importing into an existing calendar, click the Select Which Calendar down arrow and select the name of the existing calendar if it is not already displayed.
6. Click one of the Prevent Duplicates options to determine how to handle imported entries if they duplicate entries already on your calendar.
7. Click one of the Reminders options to choose how you want your reminders to be handled.
8. Click Import.

Share Your Calendar

You can share your calendar with others, such as family or those who may be collaborating with you on a project or task. You cannot share the primary calendar, however, which shows all your content. You can share your personal calendar and those that you create yourself.

You can share a calendar in two ways: you can choose Share With People You Choose, and Calendar creates an e-mail message with the link embedded in it, or you can have Calendar generate a link that you can copy and paste into an e-mail, blog, or web page that you create. When you choose Share With People You Choose, the people you choose are sent an e-mail with a link to your calendar. Calendar provides the link and you provide the e-mail addresses of collaborators. In the note part of the e-mail, you can explain why a recipient is receiving the invitation.

When you choose Get A Link, Calendar provides the link and you copy and paste it into an e-mail or another method of notifying others about your calendar.

You can make access to the calendar read-only or a full-editing version. You also can restrict access only to persons having Microsoft accounts.

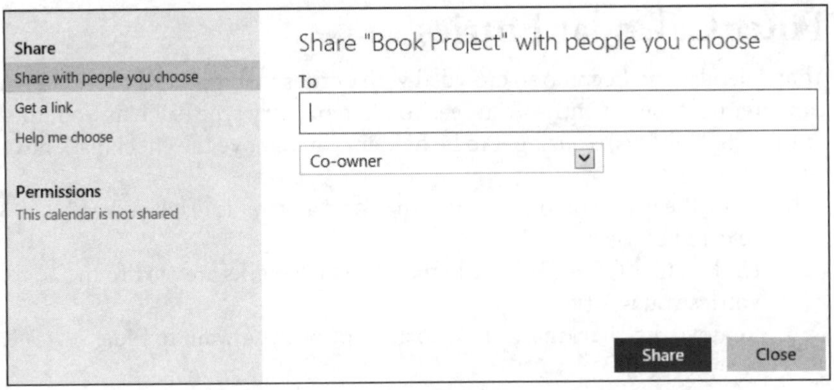

FIGURE 11-8 You can invite others to share your online calendar.

To share your calendar, follow these steps:

1. Click Share on the menu bar. A menu of the calendars you may share is displayed.
2. Select the calendar you want to share with others. A Share calendar banner is displayed, as shown in Figure 11-8.

Share by Invitation

To allow Calendar to send an e-mail with the link automatically embedded in an e-mail, do the following:

1. Click in the To text box and type the name or e-mail address of your collaborators. As you type, matching names from your People list will be displayed, from which you can select the right one. You can add multiple persons—just type another name.
2. Click the Co-owner down arrow and choose what privileges the sharing person will have. The Co-owner has total access to the calendar. The "viewing" options are the most limited.
3. Click Share. The Sharing banner will be displayed, and you'll see who can share and in which capacity.
4. Click Close.

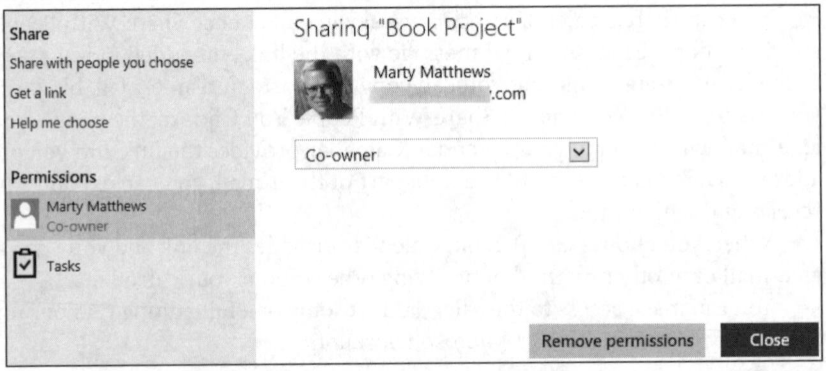

Get a Link

Using the Get A Link option, you get a link to the calendar, copy it, and then paste it wherever you want.

1. In the Calendar, click Share on the menu bar.
2. Select the calendar you want to share. The Share banner will open with the Share With People option default.
3. To have Calendar supply the URL of the calendar, click Get A Link. The Get A Link panel will be displayed.
   - Click the Show Event Details Create button to get a link that allows the sharing person to view all events in the calendar.
   - Click the Show Free/Busy Time Create button to get a link that restricts the viewer to see only your free/busy times.
   - With either option you will see a page with three link options: ability to view your calendar using a browser, permission to import your calendar into other calendar applications, and ability to view your calendar in a feed reader.
4. Highlight the link you want and press CTRL-C to copy it.

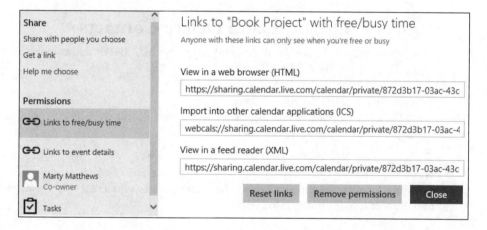

5. Click in your e-mail, web site, blog, or other medium, and press CTRL-V to paste the link.
6. Click Close to close the Links To Calendar page.

In the Get A Link page, you can reset or remove the permissions by clicking the Permissions link on the left and clicking the appropriate button on the right. Clicking Remove Permissions will remove the ability for the person to view your events or free/busy times. Clicking Reset Links will create a new set of links to send to others.

Set Calendar Options

You can set options for your calendar, such as the color, language, time format and zone, and other criteria that forms the foundation of the calendar. You can set options only for your personal and added calendars. Here's how:

1. Click the gear icon, and select Options from the menu.
2. In the Options page, go through the options and set them as desired.
3. Click Save to save your changes and return to the normal view.

Manage Your People Contacts

Use People to manage your contacts in Outlook.com and Calendar. People can come from your e-mail account, Facebook, Google, or other social networks. They are automatically imported when you activate an Outlook.com, Calendar, or People application from sources that Microsoft knows about. You can also import from other sources not known to Microsoft.

Import or Add, Edit, and Delete Contacts

Within People, you can import contacts from other sources, directly add contacts, edit and delete contacts. To open People, do the following:

1. Type **office.com** into your browser.
2. In the Office Online Home page, click the orange People icon. The People home page, displayed in Figure 11-9, will open.

Import People Contacts

If you have used other e-mail services and have contact lists associated with them, you'll probably want to import those contacts into People:

1. From your People home page, click Start Import in the right column. A list of possible import locations will be displayed, such as Google, Yahoo, Outlook, Windows Live Mail, and Other. Each location associated with a named app will give you instructions on how to export contacts from the app you chose.
   Note that if you do not see the Start Import command on the People home page, click Manage | Add People to display it.
2. To import from another location, click Other.
3. In the Imports Contact page, click Browse and search for the contact list, which must be a .csv file you exported from a name list you want to import.
4. When you find and select the contact, click Upload. The contact will be uploaded into People.

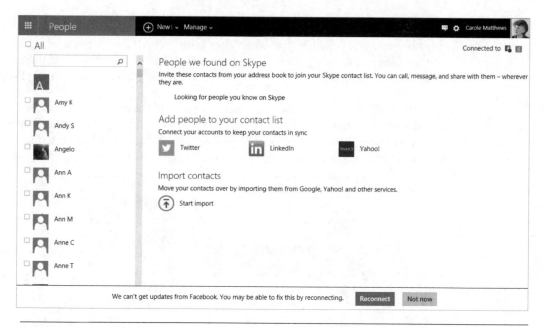

FIGURE 11-9 The People app enables you to manage your contacts for e-mail and the Calendar.

Add New Contacts

You can add people who are not part of contacts you have imported, or perhaps you just want to add a new person quickly to your list without going through the export/import process. Here's how:

1. From the People home page, click New | Contact.

2. In the Add New Contact form, fill in the information requested. If you want to add another item, such as a second name or e-mail address, click +Name or +Email, and so on.

3. When you are finished, click Save. The person's contact information is added to People.

Delete Contacts

You can remove contacts depending on where they came from. If they are imported from another service, such as a social network or e-mail contact list, you cannot delete them here. You must first delete them from the service and then the name will be removed from People.

1. From the People home page, place a checkmark next to the contact you want to delete.
2. Click Delete from the menu bar. If the contact is not connected with another service, you will see a message seeking confirmation to delete the contact. Click Delete. If the contact does come from another service, you'll see a message to that effect.

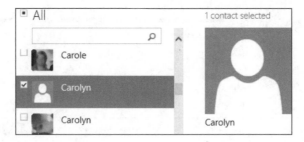

Edit Contact Information

You can change information you have on a contact. You must select only one contact at a time to edit, or the Edit command will not appear on the menu bar.

1. From the People home page, place a checkmark next to the contact you want to edit.
2. Click Edit from the menu bar.
3. In the form showing the contact information, edit the information as desired, and click Save when you're finished.

Get Rid of Duplicate Contacts

You may have duplicate entries of contacts in your People list. To check and remove duplicates, follow these steps:

1. From the People home page, click Manage | Clean Up Contacts. A scan will then run, searching for duplicate entries. If it finds any, duplicates will be deleted. If it doesn't find any, you'll be told.
2. Click Go Back on the bottom left of the screen to return to the People home page.

Manage Display of Contacts

You can change the contacts included in the display in two ways: you can filter the contacts to include or exclude imported contacts, or you can change the order of the contacts. You access these capabilities by clicking the gear icon in the menu bar, as shown in Figure 11-10.

FIGURE 11-10   You can filter contacts or rearrange the display of contacts.

Filter Contacts

To filter the contacts you want hidden, follow these steps:

1. From the menu bar, click the gear icon.
2. Click the contact services you want to hide by removing the checkmark next to them.
3. To undo the filter, place a checkmark next to the service to be included in the display.

Change Display Order

There are two ways to change the display order: by displaying either a first name/last name or last name/first name order, or by sorting either by first name or last name. The People list is by default displayed and sorted by first name/last name.

1. From the menu bar, click the gear icon.
2. From the menu,
   - Choose the display order you want.
   - Choose the sort order.

 Accessing a contact by scrolling can take a while. To make this faster, click a red letter on the left side of the People page to display all the letters of the alphabet. Click the appropriate letter to view all the contact names that start with that letter. If you have a very large People list, it might be faster to type the name in the Search text box and click the search icon (magnifying glass) to find the contact. As you type, matching names are displayed so that you can immediately find the correct one. Remove the name from the Search text box to restore the display of People.

Work with Groups

You can organize people into categories and view them more easily as a group. You might do this to send a group e-mail to all the people who are members of a club, for example. In a large People list, if you don't know the exact name of the contact, you might more easily find the information if the contact has been added to a smaller group. When you create a new group, it will be listed in the People list alphabetically. You can either scroll down to find it or type the name in the Search text box. When you click the name of the group, the contacts assigned to it are displayed, as shown in Figure 11-11.

Create a New Group

To create a new group and add people to it, follow these steps:

1. Click New | New Group.
2. In the Add New Group dialog box, click in Group Name and type the name of the group.
3. Click in the Add Member text box and begin to type the name of the person you want to add to the group. As you type, matching names will be displayed. Select the one you want.
4. When you are finished, click Save.

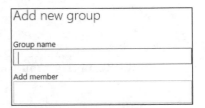

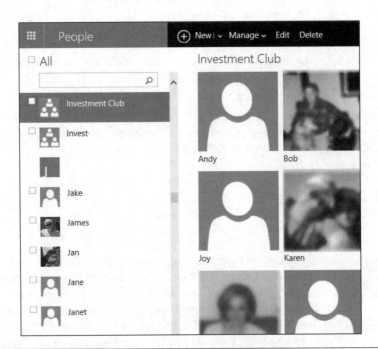

FIGURE 11-11 You can display groups of contacts.

Add People to a Group

Once a group is established you can continue to add people to it:

1. Find the group name in the alphabetic listing and place a checkmark next to it.
2. From the menu bar, click Edit.
3. In the Edit Group dialog box, click in the Add Member text box and begin to type the name of the contact you want to add to the group. As you type, matching names will be displayed. Select the one you want.
4. When you are finished, click Save.

Remove People from a Group

To remove a contact from a group, do the following:

1. Find the group name in the alphabetic listing and place a checkmark next to it.
2. From the menu bar, click Edit.
3. In the Edit Group dialog box, click the X in the lower-right corner of the person's image. The contact will be removed.
4. Click Save to save the change.

Delete a Group

Sometimes a group lasts beyond its usefulness. Or perhaps you want to start over and create a new group to replace it. For whatever reason, a group can easily be deleted. Deleting a group will not delete the contacts within it from your People list.

1. Find the group in the alphabetic listing and click it.
2. Click Delete in the menu bar.
3. Click Delete again to confirm it. The group is deleted.

Index